LUMBERJACK

LUMBERJACK

THE HISTORY, THE LORE, THE LIFE

Lauren Jarvis

STERLING
New York

CONTENTS

LUMBERJACKS: A HISTORY

Armed with axes and saws, the people who worked in the forests of North America changed the continent's historical, geographical, and cultural landscape forever

"They are a young and powerfully built race of men . . . generally unmarried, and though rude in manner, and intemperate, are quite intelligent," described author and explorer Charles Lanman in his 1856 book *Adventures in the Wilds of the United States and British American Provinces.* "They seem to have a passion for their wild and toilsome life and, judging from their dress, I should think possess a fine eye for the comic and fantastic. The entire apparel of an individual consists of a pair of gray pantaloons and two red flannel shirts, a pair of long boots, and a wool covering for the head, and all these things are worn at one and the same time."

While these observations could have been made at a taco truck in Tacoma, or a gin distillery in Dalston, these flannel-wearing menfolk aren't hipsters, millennials, or "yuccies." They are icons from another age, striding out of the forests and into eternity with shredded arms, steely eyes, and wielding a sharpened ax. Built of substance over style, they're a rare, real deal; teasing the nose with notes of winter and woodsmoke that could be bottled and sold by Tom Ford. Men who've become myth, loggers who've become legend: lumberjacks.

SPIRIT OF ADVENTURE

Just like the cowboy, the lumberjack still permeates popular culture today. As with their Wild West cousins, these iconic figures have endured for their strength, work ethic, and resilience—as well as those timelessly stylish plaid shirts.

Immortalized in books, movies, and songs, their unmistakeable look has been adopted and adapted from one generation to the next, while their pioneering spirit of adventure and connection to the great outdoors continues to inspire urban warriors to return to the woods.

The "young and powerfully built race of men" described by Charles Lanman hailed from Maine, and their "toilsome life" is the life of a logger, felling trees deep in the forests of New England during the height of the lumber boom in nineteenth-century North America.

BUILDING THE NEW WORLD

From the moment the first permanent English settlement was established in 1607 in Jamestown, Virginia, the continent's forests became its most valued resource. Trees were cut for timber to build homes and make wagons that would roll across the Great Plains to the West, while woodlands were cleared for villages and farms. The best lumber

NAME CHECK

The first known mention of the word *lumberjack* was in Canada's *Cobourg Star* newspaper in 1831, while the "lumberjill" emerged during World War II. Other terms include "shanty boy," "brush monkey," or "woodcutter," while modern lumberjacks are known as "loggers" or "timber cutters."

A lumberjack stands at the base of a partially felled tree, ca. 1900.

was reserved for the Crown and sent to England to make naval ship masts: a contentious issue which was to play a part in the American Revolution. Forested states met a growing demand throughout the 1800s, with white pine becoming the favored wood to build their new America.

Early logging camps were run by family outfits, but in the 1820s larger lumber cooperatives gained control. Pennsylvania's forests were plundered, while in New York additional land was granted to settlers who established sawmills, and its rivers flowed with logs on their way to meet them. By the 1830s, Bangor in Maine had become the world's largest shipping port for lumber, and logging crews were felling the monumental trees of America's Pacific Northwest and the pine forests of Canada.

In the mid-1800s, the process of turning wood pulp into paper came into play, which—along with mass immigration to America, the Civil War, the California Gold Rush, the rise of the railroads, and the grinding wheels of the Industrial Revolution—turned out to be bad news for trees, if not the timber barons.

RISKY BUSINESS

Despite advances in machinery, working conditions, and regulations, logging is still one of the most dangerous jobs in the world. The US Bureau of Labor Statistics' annual 2019 report on fatal occupational injuries places logging workers at number two, behind fishing and hunting workers and ahead of aircraft pilots and flight engineers.

LOGGING LEGACY

Despite being built on their breaking backs, few of the profits from the logging boom made it into the calloused hands of the lumberjacks wielding the ax or bucking the logs. Life in the lumber camps was hard. Working in isolated forests through the harsh winter months, lumberjacks slept in ice-cold, crowded bunkhouses—and pay was poor.

Long before chainsaws and harvesters were invented, even the biggest of trees were felled by hand; the name "misery whip" accurately described the discomfort of spending hours, days, and months wielding a crosscut saw. Prior to steamboats and railroads, drivers risked being crushed or drowned as they guided and rode logs along rumbling rivers to the sawmills each spring on the "log drive." Camaraderie, good humor, and strength—inner and outer—got them through.

From these remote camps and wild frontiers, the legendary lumberjacks Paul Bunyan and Big Joe Mufferaw were born. But it's the passionate, "intemperate" loggers of the lumber woods who truly left their indelible mark on North America.

WOMEN IN CAMP

Lumber camps were almost exclusively men-only zones, but by the late 1800s some women worked in the camps, usually as cooks or assistants, known as "cookees" or "flunkeys." They would prep the meals, fire up the stoves, wait on tables, and prepare lunches for men to take into the woods.

During the World Wars, with men away fighting, "loggerettes" began working in the woods and the sawmills, taking over traditionally male tasks. While many enjoyed the work, most were asked to move aside once the men returned, reverting to their roles as homemakers and mothers.

"Loggerettes" worked in the woods during the World Wars.

INDIGENOUS LUMBERJACKS

Indigenous peoples have always had a strong connection to the land, and many are striving to be responsible stewards of the forests today

Before Europeans arrived to colonize the "New World," Native people who had lived there for thousands of years already harvested trees for canoes, shelter, weapons, and art, and used bark for food, medicine, and baskets.

Indigenous people were forced to move onto farming reservations after Congress passed the Indian Appropriations Act in 1851, completely altering their way of life and restricting their ability to hunt, fish, and gather their traditional foods. Conditions on the reservations were harsh and by the end of the nineteenth century some Native Americans were working in the logging industry, traveling to find work and sending their wages back to their families on the reservations, or having their families join them. Many became team leaders thanks to their understanding of land management and natural instinct for forest work.

SAVVY STEWARDSHIP

Some communities, like the Menominee Indians of Wisconsin, began logging on their reservations. At first, the Menominee cut timber for their own use, but were later given permission to sell to outside sawmills, using the Wolf River for transportation. Between 1870 and 1890, the Indian lumberjacks cut and sold more than 88 million board feet of timber. They started a full-scale logging business, which drew in four million dollars around 1908, and opened their own sawmill in 1909.

Practicing sustainable forestry, the Menominee people have maintained a healthy forest for over 150 years, and they're still logging today. In 1994, the Menominee became the first forest management enterprise in the United States to be certified by the Forest Stewardship Council (FSC).

VALUE OF NATURE

Other Native tribes including the Klamath, Warm Springs, Siletz, Coquille, Grand Ronde, and Umatilla of Oregon are also logging using sustainable methods, restoring the diversity of flora and fauna in large areas of their tribal forests. In Canada, First Nations people, such as the Tl'azt'en Nation of British Columbia, are striving to reconcile the benefit of commercial forestry operations with traditional indigenous values and preserve their lands through sustainable practices for years to come.

"Start in the west, make your circle by taking only the sick and mature [trees], yet keep in mind by taking care of the other creatures and leaving it as you first came, as so when you make your circle to the point of start, you then will again have another stand ready for you on your next circle. For it is truly in this circle, if we take care of her, Mother Earth, for it is true that she will always be there to take care of you!"
—Chief Oshkosh, Menominee tribal leader, 1827–1858

Logging camp on the Menominee Indian Reservation, Wisconsin.

9

ON THE SKIDS

When it comes to the lumberjack dictionary, loggers left us more than "Timber!" and "Yo-Ho!"

The term *skid row*, meaning a poor city neighborhood, became popular in America during the 1930s Great Depression, but did you know that its roots lie in the logging industry?

A "skid road" was a route used to slide felled logs down to the river, or to a landing place, before they were transported to the mill. A street in Seattle, Washington, became the original urban skid road in the 1850s.

Logs felled in the surrounding forests were greased and "skidded" down a steep hill that led straight to the lumber mill, located on the Elliott Bay waterfront, overlooking Puget Sound. Now known as Yesler Way, after the mill's founder, the street runs through the Pioneer Square-Skid Road Historic District, known for its food, arts, and culture.

GRITTY CITY

In Canada, Vancouver had its own notorious skid road in what's now known as the city's Downtown Eastside. Both roads became hubs for men looking for work, and places to booze, brawl, and flop when the laboring was done. During the dark days of the Great Depression, with no work to be found, destitute men would still gather along the skid roads, with the colloquial street names and their significance morphing into the modern-day term "skid row."

Many cities still have a gritty skid row district. Old Town Chinatown in Portland, downtown Los Angeles, Kensington in Philadelphia, and the Tenderloin District in San Francisco are some of the best known, while the Bowery was considered the skid row of New York, before the regeneration of Manhattan.

Back in the forests, today's loggers are still skidding: pulling cut trees out of the forest on powerful skidders, before loading them onto trucks and transporting them to the mill.

HIP SKIDS
Skid Row was an early name used by Washington band Nirvana and is also the name of a rock band from New Jersey.

A "skid road" at a lumber camp near Wilkeson, Washington, in 1893.

CHOPPING CHAMPIONSHIPS

Traditional logging activities inspired the international sports competitions and events that modern-day lumberjacks and Jills compete in today. Here are the ones to watch

STIHL TIMBERSPORTS SERIES

Founded in 1985, this international series sees professional athletes, teams, and rookies compete in extreme woodchopping disciplines using axes, saws, and chainsaws. Men compete in six disciplines, and women compete in three.

LUMBERJACK WORLD CHAMPIONSHIPS

This event has been drawing the world's greatest lumberjacks and Jills to Hayward, Wisconsin, every year since 1960 and includes twenty-one sawing, chopping, climbing, and log-rolling competitions, plus three team contests.

SQUAMISH DAYS LOGGERS SPORTS FESTIVAL

Hosted annually in Squamish, British Columbia, this festival tests lumberjacks and Jills with a range of loggers sports, including chopping and sawing, log rolling, ax throwing, and tree topping.

SYDNEY ROYAL EASTER SHOW

First held in 1823, this annual celebration of Australian culture includes the Woodchopping & Sawing Competition which sees athletes compete in underhand, standing block, tree felling, sawing, and chainsaw events.

NEW YORK STATE WOODSMEN'S FIELD DAYS

Held each year in Boonville, New York, this homage to the lumberjack includes chopping and sawing events, along with ax throwing and log rolling.

JOHNNY APPLESEED FESTIVAL

Held annually in Sheffield, Pennsylvania, some of the world's best lumberjacks and Jills gather here to compete in chopping, sawing, and ax-throwing events.

WEBSTER COUNTY WOODCHOPPING FESTIVAL

Top choppers have been competing for the Southeastern US World Championship Woodchopper title in Webster, West Virginia, every year since 1960.

FRYEBURG FAIR

Maine's largest agricultural fair started with humble beginnings in 1851 and today draws 225,000 spectators to watch athletes compete in twenty-seven sports, including chopping, sawing, ax throwing, and log rolling.

A man competes in a log-chopping contest at a Lumbermen's Picnic, held in Cloyne, Ontario, 1947.

FELLING FASHION

The classic plaid shirt has been in style for more than 170 years, with each generation adopting the flannel for its own. We follow the evolution of the lumberjack look

The buffalo shirt has been a worldwide wardrobe staple since it was first woven by Woolrich in 1850. Like Levi's, Dr. Martens, biker jackets, or trench coats, the plaid shirt's appeal is timeless, and has been adopted and reimagined from generation to generation, with each pinning its own particular meaning to its checked lapel.

With its distinctive blocks of color and tartan-style woven patterns, plaid was conceived in Scotland, taking its name from the Gaelic word *plaide*: a heavy cloak or blanket used to keep the Highlanders warm in winter. The famous red and black shirt we know today was born in a wool mill in rural Pennsylvania. Established in 1830 by John Rich, the son of a weaver who migrated to America from Liverpool, England, in the early 1800s, the Woolrich company supplied woolen goods, like socks and blankets, to farms and lumber camps, delivering them by a mule-drawn cart.

BIRTH OF AN ICON

During its "lumberjack era" from 1830 to 1900, Woolrich was the brand of choice for loggers, hunters, and trappers, and in 1850, the mill manufactured its first Wool Buffalo Check Shirt, made from the signature buffalo plaid. "The shirt quickly became the symbol of lumberjacks and outdoorsmen, and it's remained an icon for over 170 years," says Andrea Canè, the company's creative director. "The distinct red and black color offered high outdoor visibility, and our wool was the most technical fabric of the time, crafted for maximum breathability and high performance."

"Mountain made" and "soft and supple, yet tough as iron," Woolrich's outdoor wear was durable but stylish. The company's coordinating ensemble of plaid hunting coat, breeches, and cap, which became known as the "Pennsylvania Tuxedo," was tough enough to withstand the winter weather, yet chic enough to feature in the prestigious fashion archive at New York's Metropolitan Museum of Art. Updated versions of the Tuxedo have been produced throughout Woolrich's history, along with variations on the buffalo plaid shirts and jackets.

FROM FOREST TO URBAN JUNGLE

By the 1950s, the plaid shirt had weaved its way into popular culture, with Marlon Brando famously sporting a flannel in 1954 movie *On the Waterfront*, while actors and style icons including Audrey Hepburn and Marilyn Monroe made plaid their own in tie-front shirts and pants. Even the middle classes began to follow in the giant footsteps of lumberjack folklore hero Paul Bunyan, stepping out in workwear that forged an affiliation with the great outdoors, while living increasingly suburban lifestyles.

The plaid lumberjack shirt has become a timeless wardrobe staple.

No. 220 Cap
No. 150 Coat
No. 1990 Breeches

No. 221 Cap
No. 545 Jacket
No. 1953 Breeches

No. 223 Cap
No. 258 Coat
No. 1988 Breeches

Woolrich Stag Hunting Coats

No. 150—Oxford with small Green and Red overplaid.

No. 153—Maroon and Black hunter's plaid.

No. 146—Forester's Green.

Woolrich Hunting Breeches

To Match Hunting Coats

No. 1953B—Maroon and Black hunter's plaid.

No. 1953BX—Maroon and Black hunter's plaid, double knees.

No. 1943B—Maroon and Black hunter's plaid, double seat and knees, zipper fly and legs.

No. 1990B—Oxford, small Green and Red overplaid.

No. 1972B—Dark Gray mixture.

No. 1966B—Forester's Green.

No. 1988B—Red and Black plaid.

Fine Shirts

Buffalo or Plaid Shirts

Woolrich Light Weight
Concealed Zipper Shirts

The "60" Line

Talon Fastener Shirt

No. 220 Cap
No. 126 Cruiser Coat
No. 1990 Breeches

No. 220 Cap
No. 548 Jacket
No. 1988 Breeches

Woolrich Hunting Caps

No. 220—Red leather Cap with cloth ear flaps.

No. 221—All-wool Hunter's Red and Black plaid, reversible, with ear flaps.

No. 222—Plain Red, all-wool, with ear flaps.

No. 223—Red and Black hunter's plaid, hat style, with ear flaps.

All Caps can be worn with above hunting suits, and are water-proofed.

COME AS YOU ARE

The '70s and '80s saw everyone from hippies to preppies and punks to pop stars parading in plaid, demonstrating its enduring flexibility and wearability. From the Sex Pistols to Spandau Ballet, Bowie to Bananarama, plaid has stamped an indelible mark on our culture and shaped some of music's most memorable and iconic looks. Each subculture has transformed the traditional simplicity of the design into something uniquely theirs. The shirt continued to be adopted by a diverse range of youth movements throughout the '90s. West Coast rappers including NWA and Snoop Dogg embraced oversized flannels and classic American workwear by brands like Carhartt, Ben Davis, and Dickies. In Los Angeles, the Mexican-American Chicano subculture refashioned the shirts, with men wearing them open over a T-shirt, fastening only the top button. The style is also worn by *chola* girls, a Latina subculture influenced by hip-hop, whose strong look made it into the mainstream and has been mined by stars from Gwen Stefani to Rihanna.

All the above coats and breeches are made from the same red and black 32 oz. fabric. These numbers we have put in the line to replace the all virgin wool numbers which we were compelled to discontinue on account of Government regulations. This fabric is made from 50% wool, 20% reprocessed wool, 20% reused wool and 10% rayon. All coats and shirts come with button front.

703 same make up as original 503
735 same make up as original 535
745 same make up as original 545
755 same make up as original 255

1753B same make up as original 1953B
1743B same make up as original 1943B
1783C same make up as original 1983C

Medium Small Buffalo Plaid Coat Style Shirts 13 oz.

71 shirt medium red and black check
78 shirt medium blue and black check
79 shirt medium green and black check

These shirts are made from 40% wool, 15% reprocessed wool, 10% reused wool and 35% rayon.

ABOVE: This excerpt from a Woolrich catalog showcases hunting clothing in buffalo check, a pattern first woven in 1850. **PREVIOUS SPREAD:** The plaid hunting suits produced by Woolrich became known as the "Pennsylvania Tuxedo."

In the late '50s, Pendleton Woollen Mills in the northwest made a blue plaid surf shirt, adopted by up-and-coming Californian band The Pendletones. The group continued to sport the shirts on their record covers throughout the '60s, even after changing their name and finding fame as The Beach Boys. Plaid had arrived at America's West Coast—and is still enjoying its time in the sun. "Outdoor and utilitarian clothing offers the perfect mix of durability, performance, and comfort,' says Andrea. "These design traits make wearers feel protected and prepared for anything."

The early '90s grunge scene that came out of Seattle took the plaid shirt from its logging roots in the Pacific Northwest and shot it into the stratosphere, with bands including Nirvana, Sound Garden, Alice in Chains, and Pearl Jam layering flannels over long-sleeved T-shirts. Nirvana's Kurt Cobain emerged as the scene's poster boy, although his disheveled style was born out of necessity. As a boy growing up in Washington state, Cobain was skinny and often cold, so layering helped on both counts. He was also poor for much of his life—wearing secondhand work shirts from thrift stores wasn't a contrived look.

EMPEROR'S NEW CLOTHES

When fashion house Perry Ellis dragged the grunge style off the streets and onto the catwalk in its Spring 1993 collection—with models "dressing down" in layered plaid silk shirts, raglan tees, and skirts with thousand-dollar-plus price tags—the move backfired, and not just with the working-class grunge kids.

Production was scrapped, designer Marc Jacobs was fired, and when the grunge clothing collection was sent as a marketing stunt to Cobain—who never endorsed a commercial brand in his life—he and his wife Courtney Love reacted in line with the movement's anticonsumerist ethos. "We burned it. We were punkers—we didn't like that kind of thing," Love revealed in a later interview.

Marc Jacobs brought grunge back twenty-five years later under his own label, modeled by a new generation of fashionistas. In an interview with *Elle*, he said: "We bought vintage flannel shirts for $2 on St. Marks Place and remade them out of silk. Taking something banal or vulgar and elevating it to designer status was not new. We were not the first to do it, but people got offended. They were adamant: No, you're not supposed to do that. But really, it's still happening. It's the emperor's new clothes. . . . Isn't that what fashion has always been?"

HIP, HIP TODAY

At the turn of the millennium, hipsters seized the plaid baton, ran with it into the 2010s, and are still running—or rather riding with it on their fixed-gear bikes. Perhaps more than any other subculture's adoption of the plaid shirt, the hipster scene that emerged in the early 2000s in Brooklyn full-on embraced its logging history: beards, boots, beanies, and all. Drawing on the bohemian hipster movement of the 1940s, the entrepreneurial, mainly middle-class, hip kids of Brooklyn—and soon after, London—embraced vintage clothes, retro authors, and alternative music, blending ironic nerdiness with cultivated cool.

Today, the hipster and metrosexual's hirsute love child—the lumbersexual—is found across the globe, from the coffee bars of Melbourne's Fitzroy to the microbreweries of Anchorage, Alaska. They may not be sharpening their axes to build their own cabin or log rolling their way down the river to pick up their morning cup of flat white. They might prefer hitting up hip bars than wrangling in rough 'n' ready saloons. They may just like the look and feel of a casual plaid shirt and prefer the ease of growing a robust bush of facial hair. But whatever inspires them, the new generation of buffalo-check bearers embodies the ideal of a simpler time, a connection to the natural world, and respect for authentic, hardworking lives well lived.

"The classic lumberjack shirt has really cemented itself in the fashion dialogue through its various adaptations in movies, music, and subcultures," says Andrea. "From grunge to hipsters, the aesthetic has been used by very different communities that can each relate to its unique, durable, sustainable, and nonconformist characteristics."

Like the forests where it was first put to work, the black and red plaid shirt—and the spirit it represents—is evergreen.

Grunge bands like Nirvana made the plaid flannel shirt their own in the 1990s.

WOODCHOPPING WHISKERS

If you're truly embracing the lumberjack lifestyle, there's one accessory you can't be without: a lustrous bird-nest-sized beard

While the loggers of yore likely couldn't give a hairy monkey about sporting a stylish beard, the modern-day lumbersexual wouldn't be seen dead in the forest without some well-kept facial hair. Facial hair trends may have gone in and out of fashion, but the beard's raison d'être has endured since prehistoric man was out roaming the land with a club.

Firstly, beards help keep you warm in winter—just what you need for a day out felling in the snow—while even a little fuzz will shield your face from the sun in warmer months, too. Secondly, they protect your face and will cushion any blows heading your way from a falling branch—or even a flying fist. Many believe having a beard keeps you healthy, trapping airborne cooties and toxins before they enter your mouth or nostrils. But most importantly, how much manlier does everyone look with some face foliage? Grow a beard and

you're no longer one of the smooth-shorn sheep in the herd: you, my friend, are a courageous, testosterone-fueled, mane-framed lion.

But whether you're rocking Hagrid-level hirsuteness or trying to tease the teeniest of beards from your bumfluff, these top grooming tips from the experts at the Lumberjack Beard Co. will help you to cultivate winning woodchopping whiskers.

LATHER LOVER

There are a few simple steps you can follow for a healthy, well-maintained lumberjack beard . . . and it all starts with cleanliness. An all-natural beard shampoo is a must. Regular

A robust beard has become an essential feature of the lumberjack look.

Clean-shaven lumberjacks stand in front of a sequoia tree at Converse Basin, located in California.

varieties contain chemicals that lengthen their shelf life, but using these products will actually do more damage than good, leaving your beard dry and brittle. This is why you'll see so many beard-specific shampoos and co-washes on the market. The absence of additional chemicals in natural shampoos helps to preserve natural oils, thereby retaining moisture in your beard so that it doesn't dry out and become unmanageable. Lather up your beard with a natural shampoo, then rinse it out.

> **DID YOU KNOW?**
> A healthy lifestyle can help to promote hair growth. Regular exercise, reducing stress levels, getting plenty of sleep, and eating a balanced diet will boost your beard-growing potential.

OIL IT UP

Once you've washed your beard with a natural shampoo, dab it with a towel to dry. Be careful not to rub it, as this could damage the hair at the roots. Then, before completely dry, you'll want to apply some beard oil. How much you use will depend on its length. For up to an inch (2 cm) long, four to six drops will be enough. If six inches (15 cm) or longer, you'll be looking to use between half to a full dropper's worth, to ensure the moisture from the oil reaches the tips of the hair. Squeeze the oil into your palm, then, with your fingers slightly apart, rub your palms together to spread it evenly between them. Next, brush your palms up through your beard, so that the oil reaches the skin underneath, before brushing them down the length of your beard, covering each hair with oil in the process. Finally, with a wide-toothed comb, smooth your beard into place. This will help spread the oil throughout.

HYDRATION STATION

Healthy skin equals a healthy beard, so the main purpose of the oil is to protect and hydrate the skin beneath the hair. You only need to apply beard oil once daily, first thing in the morning, to ensure both skin and beard are

Beard wax, beard balm, combs, and brushes are helpful items to have on hand when taking care of facial hair.

BEARDY LIKE BUNYAN

The lumberjack aesthetic you know and love today comes from depictions of the legendary logger Paul Bunyan, who was portrayed as a big, burly man with a beard. A typical lumberjack from the late 1800s would have been around 5 feet, 6 inches (1.7 m) tall, and was often clean-shaven. Beards attracted lice, which could be a problem in the logging camps, so big whiskers were a no-no.

well hydrated for the day ahead. For those who like to shower in the evening, you'll need to apply more beard oil afterwards. Following these two steps alone will ensure your facial hair is healthy, full, and well nourished: the most important part of beard maintenance.

BUTTER FINGERS

Once you've applied your oil, wait for at least five minutes before applying your beard balm or butter. This will allow time for the oil to work its way well into the hairs and skin beneath. While beard butter can be used at any time of the day, its nourishing qualities can add much-needed moisture to your beard throughout the night. Balm on the other hand is hardier and more robust, and is more commonly used to offer protection against the elements. Both are applied the same way. Scrape out roughly a thumbnail-sized amount of either onto your palm. With your fingers spread slightly apart, rub your palms together until the product becomes more liquid, then apply it to your beard. Balms will take longer to emulsify than butters because of the higher concentration of beeswax or other holding agents used to make them. When your palms are thoroughly covered, run your fingers up through your beard, before running your palms down the length of your beard to create that protective shield.

BLOW YOUR BRISTLES

For a more stylized beard, use the cold setting on a hairdryer to set it. Hold the device about 6 inches (15 cm) from your face, making sure to point the nozzle down the length of your beard only. Use a comb or brush to smooth your beard hair into place, straightening out any unruly curls in the process. The cold air will help to set the beeswax, giving you a neat, well-groomed look. You'll need to trim it occasionally to keep it in tip-top shape, so invest in a good pair of beard scissors, plus a beard-shaping tool to help with any tricky curves and angles. Now off a-lumbering you go.

HOW TO BE A WORLD CHAMPION LUMBERJACK

The Stihl Timbersports series sees some of the world's best athletes go head-to-head in extreme wood-cutting competitions. Current world champion Brayden Meyer reveals what it takes to be the ultimate lumberjack

Woodchopping has come a long way since the first competition between two axmen in Ulverstone, Tasmania, in 1870. Betting $50 on who could chop 3-foot (91 cm) standing blocks the fastest, Joseph Smith and Jack Briggs unknowingly sparked what has become a 150-year-old sports tradition.

Competitive woodchopping was formally recognized in 1891, with the establishment of the United Australasian Axeman's Association and the inaugural Woodchopping World Championship, held at Atkinson's saleyards in Latrobe, Australia. The winner was Tom Reeves of Barrington, who chopped through a 2-foot (61 cm) standing block in 6 minutes, 22.5 seconds. The Australian Axeman's Hall of Fame and Timberworks marks the spot today. The first true World Championship Series was staged in Ulverstone in 1970, drawing teams from Australia, New Zealand, Canada, and the United States, won by Tasmania's George Foster.

Australia is still leading the woodchopping charge today, with Victoria's Brayden Meyer holding the World Championship title in the men's division, and Australia's "Chopperoos" holding the title in the team division of the Stihl Timbersports Series.

EXTREME ATHLETES

Stihl Timbersports began in 1985, with the earliest events broadcast from a field in Wisconsin—historically, one of the most prolific lumber-producing states in the US. Today, the series has a massive global following and is broadcast on TV networks around the world, attracting top athletes to take part in regional, national, and international competitions, with their roots deeply entwined in logging tradition.

Brayden Meyer competes in the springboard competition at the 2019 Stihl Timbersports World Championship in Prague.

Andreas Stihl invented the first modern electric chainsaw in 1926, signaling the move away from human-powered axes and crosscut saws, but all three feature in the series.

The men's professional division features six disciplines: three with an ax (underhand chop, springboard, and standing block chop) and three with saws—single buck (using a crosscut saw), stock saw (using a heavy-duty chainsaw), and hot saw (a free class using customized chainsaws). The women's professional division includes three disciplines: the underhand chop, single buck, and stock saw.

The winner is the athlete or team that collects the most points over the course of the competition. There are also rookie, intermediate, and team divisions, and a challenging Champion's Trophy, where athletes complete four disciplines (underhand chop, single buck, standing block chop, and stock saw), back-to-back.

Each discipline tests the endurance, strength, and technical ability of the athletes against the clock, with the world's best woodcutters obliterating logs (from sustainably grown trees) in seconds, setting new world records faster than you can, er, swing an ax.

FAMILY TREE

Reigning world champion Brayden stormed away with the title at the 2019 Championships in Prague, Czech Republic, three years after becoming the Champion's Trophy holder in 2016. A fourth-generation woodchopper from Broadford, Australia, Brayden has timbersports in his blood and, when he's not competing around the world, works as a logger in the eucalyptus forests of Victoria's Central Highlands. "My dad and uncles are all axmen, and I've grown up working with wood and handling chainsaws and axes," says Brayden. "I entered my first local wood-chopping competition aged nine, but I've had an ax in my hand pretty much since I could walk."

Brayden was introduced to the Stihl Timbersports series by his uncle, Brad Turner, who's also a champion athlete. Brayden won his first national title in 2015, aged only nineteen—the same year he took bronze in the World Championships. Along with his individual titles, he's also a five-time team world

champion, thanks to wins with the Australian Chopperoos, and holds the current world record in the underhand chop event with a time of just 12.39 seconds.

Now twenty-six, Brayden is at the top of his game, winning the Australian virtual championships in 2020. At 6 feet, 2 inches (1.9 m) and weighing in at an impressive 265 pounds

A competitor in a woodchopping event at the Gawler Show, South Australia, 1941.

(120 kg), he's a force to be reckoned with, combining incredible strength with stamina and agility.

"My job is very physical, which definitely helps with my fitness, but I also do a lot of running and cycling. Repetition is the best training, so I do two sessions of two or three hours every week, where I practice the timbersports disciplines," he says. "I've always believed that if you work hard at something, you'll see the results and earn the rewards."

Brayden shares his tips for smashing six extreme competitions:

STANDING BLOCK CHOP
Competitors must use their ax to chop through both sides of a block of wood in the fastest time. The timber measures around 1 foot (30 cm) in diameter and is anchored vertically in a metal stand.

WORLD RECORD HOLDER
The United States' Matt Cogar shattered the record at the 2018 event in Liverpool, with a time of 11.03 seconds.

WHAT'S THE HISTORY?
This discipline closely simulates the action of felling a tree. It requires powerful, fast, and accurate strikes with the ax.

HOW TO BE THE BEST
Brayden says: "Aim to strike the block at 45-degree angles and don't hold the ax too close to your body. Old timers say 'aim for the grass' for your up hits and 'reach for the sky' for the down hits. Put everything you've got into your swing, develop a rhythm, and focus on the point you want to hit or you'll miss it."

UNDERHAND CHOP
The athlete stands on top of a horizontally mounted 2-foot-long (61 m) tree trunk, which measures just over a foot in diameter. At the starting signal, they must chop through the log from both sides with their ax, cutting the log completely in two as fast as they can. Steel mesh socks to protect the feet and shins are a must.

Brayden takes on the underhand chop at 2019's Stihl Timbersports World Championship in Prague.

WORLD RECORD HOLDER
Australia's Brayden Meyer chopped his way into the record books with a time of just 12.39 seconds at the 2015 event in Poznan, Poland. Australia's Amanda Beans holds the women's world record, with a time of 36.16 seconds, set at the 2019 Australian World Championships.

J. H. Matheson competes at the Royal Adelaide Show at Wayville, South Australia, in 1948.

WHAT'S THE HISTORY?

This discipline replicates the action of bucking felled trees into manageably sized logs, before they were hauled from the forest and transported to the mill.

HOW TO BE THE BEST

Brayden says: "Most people start off doing the underhand chop, as it's one of the safest timbersports disciplines. Focus on honing your timing and hand-eye coordination. Once you've nailed your technique, it's about making sure you have the stamina to keep going."

SPRINGBOARD

At the starting signal, competitors use their ax to chop a 4-inch-deep (10 cm) pocket into a vertically mounted log at shoulder height. Slotting a wooden "springboard" into the gap, they stand on it and chop a second shoulder-height pocket into the log, slotting another board into it. Standing on the second, 6 feet (1.8 m) above the ground, they must cut through a block of wood at the top of the log. The first to do it, wins.

WORLD RECORD HOLDER

Canada's Stirling Hart set the current record with a time of 35.67 seconds at the 2016 World Championships in Stuttgart, Germany.

WHAT'S THE HISTORY?

This technique was used by loggers to make cutting platforms, allowing them to chop above the hard root base or spur of a tree, which could be several feet tall.

HOW TO BE THE BEST

Brayden says: "It's important to work on building up your leg strength and agility for this event, as you need to be quick jumping up onto the boards. Bike riding is a good way to get your legs in shape, but be sure to keep practicing your chopping technique so you become faster, stronger, and more accurate, too."

SINGLE BUCK

The athlete uses a 5-foot, 8-inch (1.7 m) to 6-foot, 4-inch (1.9 m) crosscut saw to cut a complete wooden disc or "cookie" off a horizontally-fixed, white pine tree trunk, approximately 1.5 feet (45 cm) in diameter, in the shortest time possible. The competitor can spray the saw with oil before they start to help with lubricity.

WORLD RECORD HOLDER

Canadian Ben Cumberland sawed through a log in 12.94 seconds at the 2019 Prague World Championships.

Brayden cuts a "cookie" at the Stihl Timbersports World Championship 2019.

New Zealand's Jason Wynyard set a record of 9.39 seconds at the 2007 US International Championships, which he held for twelve years before a rule change, which stopped assistants aiding athletes in the event. Germany's Svenja Bauer set a new women's world record (with assistant) of 16.83 seconds at the 2014 German Women Jungheinrich Cup.

WHAT'S THE HISTORY?

While the saws used in the competition are made for racing, they're based on the design of the "misery whip": the traditional two-man crosscut saw, once widely used for cutting logs.

HOW TO BE THE BEST

Brayden says: "Don't let the length of the saw put you off: This isn't as hard as it looks once you get the hang of it. Let the saw do the work, but use your legs, arms, and hips to keep it moving and sawing freely."

STOCK SAW

At the signal, competitors pick up the idling MS661 chainsaw and cut two cookies of a specified thickness from a marked area of a horizontally mounted poplar log. The fastest competitor to perform one downward and one upward cut on the 16-inch-diameter (41 cm) log wins.

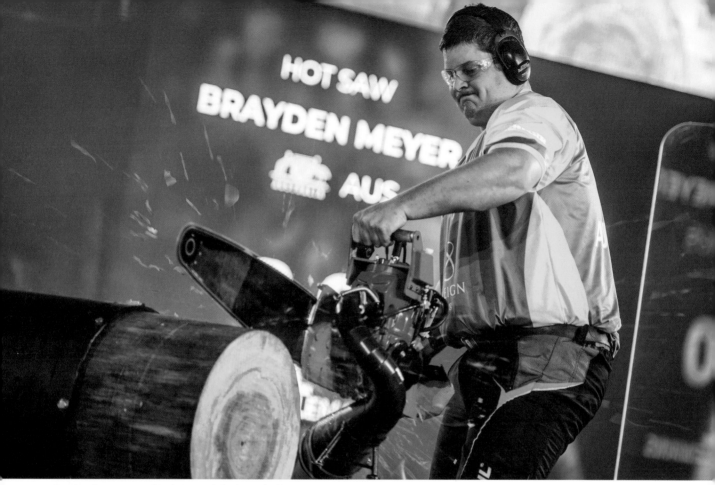

Brayden demonstrates his chainsaw skills during the hot saw competition at the 2019 Stihl Timbersports Championship in Prague.

WORLD RECORD HOLDER

Marcin Juskowski of Poland set a new record at the 2020 Polish Championships, with a time of 9.51 seconds.

Alrun Uebing from Moschheim in Germany holds the women's world record of 9.60 seconds, set at 2020's German Amarok Cup.

WHAT'S THE HISTORY?

This event demonstrates the chainsaw skills of the athlete—and requires the strength, accuracy, and control shown by lumberjacks using these powerful tools in the forest.

HOW TO BE THE BEST

Brayden says: "Using a chainsaw can be daunting at first, so take your time getting to know how it feels and works. Make sure you have a good grip on the handles and start sawing slowly, building your pace over time. This discipline is about speed, but also controlled and accurate cutting."

HOT SAW

This is the finale of any Stihl event. Athletes must start the saw and cut three cookies of a specified thickness from a horizontally mounted tree trunk, approximately 1.5 feet

(46 cm) in diameter, as quickly as possible. The first cut is downward, followed by upward, then downward again. The powerful, custom-built chainsaws are made with 250- to 400-cubic-centimeter single-cylinder engines, taken from dirt bikes, jet skis, or snowmobiles. They can weigh up to 66 pounds (30 kg), have a chain speed of 155 miles per hour (250 km/h), and are very loud.

WORLD RECORD HOLDER
Dirk Braun from Germany set the current record at the 2016 German National Championships, with a scorching time of just 5.2 seconds.

WHAT'S THE HISTORY?
The crowd's favorite event, and one of the most challenging for competitors, the hot saw competition draws on engineering skills, as well as chainsaw ability. Like the resourceful lumberjacks of the past, athletes modify their tools, or work with engineers, to get maximum results.

HOW TO BE THE BEST
Brayden says: "My saw comes from the US and it's custom-made with a 330-cubic-centimeter engine. It weighs around 66 pounds (30 kg), but once it's going, I don't really notice the weight. These saws aren't for beginners: they're a bit like having a powerful motorbike in your hand! Start using a regular chainsaw first and once you've mastered that and feel confident, move on to the hot saw.

"During the competition season there's usually a chopping event each weekend and I love it. I've been brought up with the sport, and it's a great community: we're competitive, but we support each other, too."

EAT LIKE A WORLD CHAMP

**Want to know what a world champion lumberjack eats to power all that chopping?
Take a look at Brayden's daily food diary**

BREAKFAST
2 pieces toast with butter and Vegemite
or strawberry jam

SNACK
Banana with yogurt or an apple

LUNCH
2 chicken or beef and salad wraps

DINNER
Honey mustard chicken with rice
or spaghetti with meatballs

DRINKS
½ gallon (2 l) water

TREATS
2 cans of beer

TOOLS OF THE TRADE

Today's high-tech harvesters and forwarders can cut and clear trees with ease, but in the 1800s, logging with human-powered hand tools was back-breaking work. Here's a guide to the essential old-school lumberjack hardware

AX

The essential and most iconic of all lumberjack accessories, the ax was the primary tool used for felling trees until saws became the preference in the 1880s. Loggers had the choice of two heads: single- or double-bitted, with many different head shapes (see pages 40–41 for examples) and weights to choose from. Wider blades are better for chopping softwoods, and narrow blades are better for hardwoods. Axes were also used for cutting the branches off trees, known as "limbing."

CROSSCUT SAW

Still widely used around the world, one- or two-person cross-cut saws—measuring from 4 to 16 feet (1.2–4.9 m)—are designed to cut across the wood grain. Felling saws for cutting down trees have a concave back, and are lighter and more flexible with a narrower blade; while bucking saws for cutting trees into logs have a straight back and are heavier and stiffer, with a broader blade. Loggers call the two-person saw the "misery whip," reflecting the hardship of a day felling trees by hand in the forest.

TWICE AS TOUGH

On a double-bitted ax, one edge is usually sharp for chopping, and the other is "stunt" or thicker for work where it may hit metal, stone, or tree knots.

BOW SAW

First developed in Sweden, the smaller, one-person bow saw—also known as a buck- or Swede saw—cuts smaller logs, less than 10 inches (25 cm) in diameter. It was the tool of choice for cutting pulpwood—used for making paper products—in Canada and the United States.

WEDGE

Essential for felling, bucking, and splitting wood, wedges lift the tree, preventing it from sitting back when it's being felled. They also reduce binds on the saw during bucking, allowing the tool to continue to move freely. In the early 1800s, lumberjacks used old ax handles or wooden wedges to help fell a tree, with steel and iron varieties coming into play towards the end of the century. They usually measure up to 12 inches (30 cm) and are 1 inch (2 cm) thick at the head (splitting wedges are usually thicker and longer).

A logger uses a crosscut saw in Malheur National Forest in Oregon, 1942.

ABOVE: Two lumberjacks pose with a crosscut saw, axes, and a mallet in Wisconsin, ca. 1900. OPPOSITE: Two men use cant hooks to move a fallen tree near Effie, Minnesota, 1937.

PEAVEY

This long pole (also called a stock or handle) has a metal spike or pick at the end and a lever to help grab and turn logs. Named for Joseph Peavey, the blacksmith who invented the tool that revolutionized the logging industry in 1857, the Peavey Manufacturing Company still makes them today.

CANT HOOK

Similar to a peavey but, instead of a point at the end, fitted with a metal thimble with a bill and a lever. Used more frequently at the landing in the forest or the mill—rather than on the river—its primary use is for rolling logs.

PIKE POLE

This wooden tool, with a straight metal spike and hook at the end, was used to transport logs along the river and construct timber rafts.

PULP HOOK

A short, one-handed device, used for moving small logs of pulpwood. The hook is made of steel with an oval handle and is useful for handling frozen wood.

CALK OR CAULK BOOTS

This tough, spike-soled footwear gave better traction when logging in damp forests, and riding the logs on rumbling rivers during the spring drive. The boots are still worn by forestry workers today.

HOOKED ON THE RIVER

In the heyday of the river drives, Maine's Peavey Manufacturing Company made twelve different styles of hooks. The last Maine river drive was in 1976, when trains and trucks took over transporting logs to the mill.

BUTT OR POLL
Blunt back of
ax-head, helps
with balance and
control

HEAD
"Business end" of the ax,
usually made from stainless
or carbon steel, comes in
many shapes and sizes

BELLY
Curve in the handle's
upper section

CHEEK
Smooth section of
each side of the head

SHOULDER
Sturdy region lying just
below the butt or poll

WEDGE
Made of metal
or wood, this
helps to secure
the head inside
the eye

BEARD
Underside of the head
between the handle and heel

BEVEL OR CHISEL
Angled, polished
section near the bit that
determines the angle of
approach into the wood

EYE
Hole where the
handle fits into
the head

BIT OR EDGE
Sharp, cutting side of
the head

TOE
Upper corner of the bit

HEEL
Bottom corner of the bit

KNOB OR BELL
Very end of the ax handle

WEDGE ALERT
The phrase "to fly off the handle"—meaning to lose emotional control—came from the uncontrolled way an ax head can fly from its handle if it isn't properly wedged.

HANDLE
Traditionally made from hardwoods like ash or hickory, some are crafted from steel or durable synthetic materials including fiberglass

THROAT
Curved lower section of the handle

ANATOMY OF AN AX

There's more to this tool than just a head and a handle—many elements are named for body parts. Here's an in-depth dissection of the lumberjack's trusty chopper

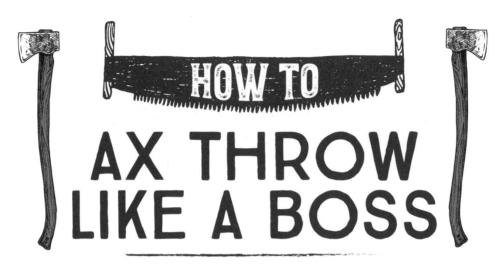

HOW TO
AX THROW LIKE A BOSS

Yo-ho! It's time to ax throw. And nobody is more qualified to help you hit the bullseye than seven-time world champion lumberjack Darren Hudson

No activity is better at hurling us back to our primordial roots than throwing an ax. One of the world's earliest known tools, teardrop-shaped axes dating back 1.8 million years have been excavated in Lake Turkana in northwest Kenya, while the first ax with a handle, found in northwestern Australia's Windjana Gorge, is up to 49,000 years old.

The ax was one of the lumberjack's essential tools—European versions were used by early loggers, but weightier designs were needed to quickly fell trees and clear lands, so blacksmiths began to counterweight the back of the ax head, increasing the cut on each stroke. The iconic American double-bitted ax reared its head around the time of the Civil War. Symmetrical with wide blades either side of the wooden handle, this was the tool of legendary lumberjack Paul Bunyan, with one bit often used for heavy work like splitting and the other finely honed for cutting.

Ax-throwing champion, seven-time log-rolling world champion, and twelve-time Canadian champion log-roller Darren Hudson is a fifth-generation lumberjack, who keeps up his family traditions logging pine and spruce on their land in Nova

Scotia. A self-confessed ax maniac (in the best possible sense), Darren also runs Wild Axe Productions, which offers wannabe lumberjacks and Jills the chance to learn the skills of Nova Scotia's expert woodsmen in its Lumberjack AXEperience. He's also an in-demand ax designer, owner of The Timber Lounge ax-throwing bar in Moncton, and has even created a pilsner called Wild Axe with local craft brewing company Boxing Rock.

"My family have been driving logs down the Barrington River since 1883," says Darren. "And I've been log rolling since I was in the womb, because my mother used to compete in lumberjack competitions before I was born. I first competed aged nine, and I was tall, skinny, and fast, so I was good at tree climbing and log rolling. But the beauty of ax throwing is that you can still do it in the twilight of your career—well into your eighties if your shoulders hold up—because it requires flexibility and coordination, rather than strength."

Champion lumberjack Darren Hudson wields his custom-designed Wild Axe Dragon.

Tempted? Here are Darren's six tips to becoming an ax aficionado:

1. There's more than one good way to throw an ax, and as we're all built differently, everybody will throw in their own style. You'll discover what works best for you the more you practice.

2. Always make sure the area is clear of people before throwing.

3. Square up to the target and plant your feet firmly on the ground, shoulder-width apart with your best foot slightly forward, which will help you to feel balanced. Throwing the ax with two hands is easier for beginners. Stand behind the throwing line and position yourself directly in line with the bullseye. If you'd rather throw with one hand, you'll need to line up the shoulder of your throwing arm instead.

4. It helps to have a good eye, so make sure you stay focused on the bullseye at the center of the target during your throw.

5. Try not to hold onto the handle too hard, as this makes it harder to let the ax go and keep it on target. If you're throwing with two hands, bring the ax directly back over your head, like you're throwing a ball. Then power forward with your body, swinging your ax overhead. Fully extend your arms and release when your hands are pointed at the bullseye. To throw with one hand, bring the ax back past your ear until it nearly touches your shoulder, keeping it straight. Then bring your arm forward and release the ax when the handle is vertical in front of you. A clean and consistent release is the key to success.

6. Work on your body's flexibility to ensure you have the proper range of motion to maintain your balance throughout the entirety of your throw. And most of all, enjoy it!

HOW DO I GET STARTED?

For your first foray into ax throwing, go to a facility where a professional will show you the ropes, they have good safety standards in place, and you can use their axes. The sharper the tool you use, the safer it will be, as it's more likely to stick in the target. If you decide to take the sport further, you'll need a special ax for throwing, rather than a general one from a hardware store, choosing one that's right for your body build.

THE COMPETITION

Competitors must stand behind the throwing line and throw their ax at a wooden target, 20 feet (6.1 m) away. If a thrower steps over the line before or during their throw, they score zero. The target consists of rings worth 1–5 points, scoring higher the closer your ax lands to the bullseye. Only the fore-bit of the double-bit ax can score a hit, and it must stick into the target area. The fore-bit only needs to touch the line separating two scoring areas to win the higher points. The winner is whoever has the best score after three goes, although playing the best of five or six throws is also common.

LEFT: Darren continues the lumberjack legacy of his uncle Stanley Scott, who shares his stories in "A Lumberjack's Tale" (pages 50–53).
OPPOSITE: Coaches at the Timber Lounge in Moncton, New Brunswick, demonstrate how to throw an ax.

HEADS UP!

Ax heads come in many
different shapes and sizes,
with patterns often named
for the region where they
were first used

DOUBLE-BIT AX HEADS

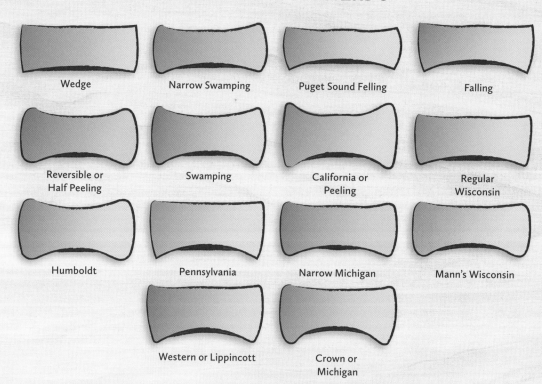

Wedge

Narrow Swamping

Puget Sound Felling

Falling

Reversible or
Half Peeling

Swamping

California or
Peeling

Regular
Wisconsin

Humboldt

Pennsylvania

Narrow Michigan

Mann's Wisconsin

Western or Lippincott

Crown or
Michigan

SINGLE-BIT AX HEADS

Southern Kentucky

Kentucky

Michigan

Dayton

Regular Wisconsin

Mann's Wisconsin

Turpintine

Baltimore Kentucky

Baltimore Jersey

Rockaway

Western Crown or Ohio

Hoosier or Zeek

Wedge

Falling

Yankee

California Yankee

Connecticut

Rafting

Maine

Half Wedge

Virginia

Long Island

Phila-jersey

New England

Narrow Michigan

Delaware or Wide-Bit Dayton

North Carolina

Georgia

HOW TO
MAKE AN AX

Humans have been using them for millennia, but how do you forge an ax of champions? Legendary blacksmith Hayward Meisner shares his expert tips for transforming metal into something magic

The essential lumberjack's tool needs to be as strong as the person wielding it, and making a great ax takes skill, patience, and passion. Blacksmith Hayward Meisner has all these qualities in spades, producing ornamental ironwork and traditionally crafted axes from his ironworks forge in Lockeport, Nova Scotia.

Hayward was first introduced to metalworking by a friend who was visiting the region for the summer. "I tried it, and from the moment I started working with metal, I was completely hooked," says Hayward. So hooked, that he switched careers from electrician to blacksmith, building and equipping his own forge and shop forty years ago. Working with both traditional and modern tools, Hayward is helping to keep historic crafts alive, while inspiring a younger generation of local blacksmiths to take up the trade at the same time.

"It's a privilege to work with tools that haven't changed for generations," he says. "Like the anvil, the ax is a perfectly designed implement with so many uses. I'll never tire of forging a good ax."

LOOK SHARP

It's important to sharpen your ax with a slow-turning grinding wheel, as a fast-turning belt could heat up the steel enough to affect the tempering of the blade.

ARM'S LENGTH

The length of handle on your ax should measure roughly the same length as your arm, from the fingertips to the top.

Hayward demonstrates how to forge an ax:

1. First, you need to decide on the weight of your ax and choose your steel accordingly. For a 3.5-pound (1.6 kg) ax, you'll need around 3.75 pounds (1.7 kg) of carbon steel—the carbon ensures the ax will be hard. Next, holding the steel in a vice, mark a hole where the eye of the ax will sit—this is important for the symmetry of your tool. I'm making a double-bit, so the eye will sit in the center. For a single-bit ax, the eye will be closer to the butt.

2. Next, you need to heat the steel block in the forge, using iron tongs. Working with steel requires extreme heat. For me, a good forging temperature is between 1,000–1,800°F (538–982°C), after which the steel will melt. Coal is used traditionally, which turns to "coke" when it's burned on a fire, releasing the intensity of heat you'll need to work with the metal.

3. Holding the steel with tongs, use a sharp punch to cut through the metal and make the eye. This is done from both sides, so the hole meets in the middle.

4. Use a drift (a tapered metal rod) to widen the eye until it's big enough to accommodate the handle, carefully knocking it through the steel with a mallet. This doesn't remove any steel but moves it so the sides of the block will bulge a little.

5. Turning the block on its side, use a hammer to correct the alignment of the steel, before doing the same on the other side, working both sides equally. At this stage, the steel is like putty or clay, but if it gets too cold, it will no longer be malleable.

6. Next, it's time to fan the blade, hammering it and pushing the steel to form the shape of your ax head, ensuring both bits are symmetrical if you're making a double-bit ax.

7. Now your ax is really starting to take shape. Once the steel changes color from yellow to cherry red you know, it's starting to cool down, although it's still extremely hot.

8. It's time to quench the ax using water or oil. A red-hot piece of steel plunged into water will quickly make the water boil away from the metal, so the steel will take longer to cool. Oil doesn't heat up as quickly, so it cools the metal faster. Quenching leads to hardening of the metal, which makes it too brittle to work with, so the metal needs to be tempered.

Tempering uses a more controllable heat source, like a propane flame. This important process resoftens the metal just the right amount, so it's no longer too hard to be brittle and break, or so soft that the blade edge will bend over or mash. As you run the flame over the metal, you'll see the color change from straw to purple, to blue, and then to deep blue, which means it's at the optimum temperature for tempering. If you see gray, you've heated the steel too much.

9. Once tempered, the ax head should have a heat bath for around an hour at 400°F (200°C)—a nice spa treatment—which allows the molecules to settle into position. Then the handle is inserted and fixed in the eye with a wedge. This Dragon Ax, designed by champion ax thrower Darren Hudson, is marked with scallop shapes made on a die grinder, so it's as beautiful to look at as it is to use.

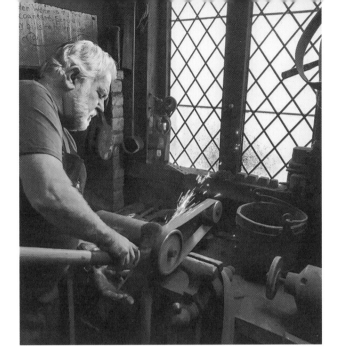

ABOVE: Hayward at work in his forge. **BELOW:** The world's largest ax is in Nackawic, named the Forestry Capital of Canada in 1991. Made from 55 tons (50 metric tons) of stainless steel, the base serves as an events stage. A time capsule is embedded in the 23-foot-long (7 m) ax-head.

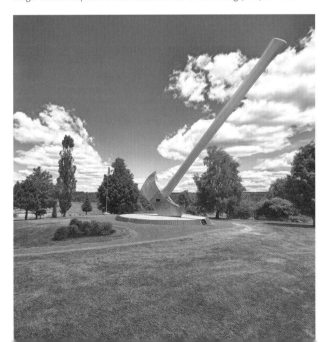

THE LEGENDARY LOGGER
PAUL BUNYAN

Born from forest folklore, larger-than-life lumberjack Paul Bunyan and his companion, Babe the Blue Ox, have become icons of American culture

Even if you've never heard of the world's most famous lumberjack, Paul Bunyan, you've probably seen him. The giant axman has popped up in movies such as the Coen brothers' *Fargo*, welcoming visitors entering the town of Brainerd, and Andrés Muschietti's big-screen adaptation of Stephen King's novel *It*, when a statue of the logger wielding a giant peavey comes to life in Derry in *Chapter Two*. Bunyan also stars in the less terrifying animated eponymous musical by Walt Disney. And if you're ever road-tripped around America, you'll have likely driven past him a few times, too.

The original statue that influenced King's book can be found in Bangor, Maine. Made of steel and fiberglass and standing over 30 feet (9.1 m) tall, it was erected in 1959 and is believed to be the largest statue of Bunyan in the world. Many others exist, the super-sized, plaid-shirt-wearing woodsman looming large in towns across the United States, from Bemidji, Minnesota (home to the oldest statue, dating from 1937) to Klamath in California, where a 49-foot (15 m) animatronic version waves his hand at visitors to the Trees of Mystery nature attraction, with a booming: "Hello there!"

MAN OR MYTH?

But how did the legend of the towering tree cutter grow to such epic proportions? Tall tales featuring bumper-sized Bunyan and his equally brawny blue ox, Babe, first emerged in North America's early logging camps. According to *Out of the Northwoods: The Many Lives of Paul Bunyan* by author Michael Edmonds, the earliest reliable account was from a lumber camp in Wisconsin in the winter of 1885–1886. As workers moved from season to season and state to state, the tales they told moved with them, becoming bigger and bolder with each retelling.

While some believe the legend of Bunyan could be based on a real-life lofty lumberjack—both Bangor in Maine and Bemidji in Minnesota claim to be his birthplace, and there are records of woodsmen recounting firsthand encounters with Paul and his crew—the stories of his superhuman size and endeavors place him firmly in the fictional realm. Even the burliest of shanty boys would have struggled to carve the Grand Canyon with their ax, dig out the Great Lakes as watering troughs for Babe, or create 10,000 lakes from their footprints as they strode around Minnesota chasing a big, blue ox.

Bunyan allegedly created the Mississippi River, when a water tank he was pulling developed a leak, and tales of Paul's birth were pretty epic, too. It took five giant storks to deliver him as a baby, he could fit into his father's clothes at one week old, and the

PAUL BUNYAN DAY
So famous is the lumbering logger, that he even has his own special day—June 28. If there's ever a time to cook up some pancakes or throw an ax, this is it.

A giant 31-foot-tall (9.4 m) Paul Bunyan statue greets visitors to Bangor, Maine.

The Paul Bunyan and Babe the Blue Ox statues in Klamath, California, are visible from Highway 101.

family needed ten cows to supply enough milk to keep him happy. He ate forty bowls of oatmeal a day, and once, rolling over, he caused an earthquake. The woods were the safest place for the rapidly growing boy, and here he felled trees at superhuman speed and developed a passion for pancakes, or flapjacks, cooked on a vast griddle in a gargantuan kitchen.

OUT OF THE WOODS

Reference to the logging legend first made it into print in 1893, when "Paul Bunion" was mentioned in Michigan's *Gladwin County Record*, while Minnesota's *Duluth News Tribune* was the first to publish a story about the lumberjack in an article entitled "Caught on the Run" in 1904. With news of the woodsman's incredible antics spreading, *Outer's Book*

magazine ran an article featuring three Bunyan tales, called "Some Lumberjack Myths," in 1910. Written by James Rockwell and reprinted in *The Washington Post*, its popularity led to Rockwell writing sixteen more stories about Paul and his ox, who was allegedly blue due to North Dakota's notorious "winter of the blue snow"—a treacherous cold snap that struck in 1886–1887. Also in 1910, reporter James MacGillivray's story "The Round River Drive" was published in the *Detroit News Tribune*, which told tales from *Legends of Paul Bunyan, Lumberjack* by K. Bernice Stewart and Homer A. Watt, published in 1916—the first scholarly collection of stories that had been circulating around the logging camps for thirty years or more. Through interviews with lumber workers, the authors drew together anecdotes from a range of states, including

Wisconsin, Michigan, Minnesota, Washington, and Oregon. Describing him as "a powerful giant, seven feet tall and with a stride of seven feet," they confirmed that "he was famous throughout the lumbering districts for his great physical strength" but deemed some of the loggers' yarns "too coarse for publication."

INTO THE SPOTLIGHT

The Red River Lumber Company of Minneapolis seized on the character's growing popularity and began publishing promotional brochures featuring Bunyan in 1914—the first entitled *Introducing Mr. Paul Bunyan of Westwood, California*. In the hands of Minnesotan copywriter William B. Laughead, who went on to produce *Tales about Paul Bunyan, Vol. II* and *The Marvelous Exploits of Paul Bunyan*, the woodsman became imbued with increasingly superhuman qualities, while his blue ox was christened Babe. Pictured for the first time, Red River trademarked Laughead's illustration of Bunyan's head and began to use his name in business dealings. Now with broader appeal, this marketable version epitomized the big, burly, hardworking woodcutter, complete with check shirt, beard, and a double-bit ax: The classic lumberjack image was born.

Featured in hundreds of books for both children and adults, and inspiring songs, cartoons, poems, and even an eponymous operetta—written by Anglo-American poet W. H. Auden and British composer Benjamin Britten and premiered in New York in 1941—the legendary lumberjack's tales have not only endured but are also endlessly evolving, woven as firmly into the fabric of American folklore as Bunyan's buffalo plaid shirt.

MUFFLER MAN

A giant statue of Bunyan was erected in 1962 to promote the Paul Bunyan Cafe on Route 66 in Flagstaff, Arizona. Produced by Bob Prewitt, founder of the Californian International Fiberglass company, this was the first of hundreds of giant "muffler men" built in the next decade, used to advertise stores, goods, and services across the United States and Canada.

HIT THE ROAD

Minnesotans are mad for all things Bunyan. The state's Paul Bunyan Scenic Byway is a 54-mile (87 km) scenic route encompassing hiking and walking trails, beaches, parks, and gardens. Meanwhile, the 120-mile (193 km) Paul Bunyan Trail is Minnesota's longest biking trail.

A 1949 advertisement for Timken Detroit Axles shows Paul Bunyan carrying a log.

A LUMBERJACK'S TALE

Freezing winters, soaking-wet socks, and pilfering raccoons—take a journey down the Barrington River in Canada's Nova Scotia with Stanley Scott, 88, who recalls what life was like as a lumberjack in the 1940s

Biting cold and roaring, the river was raging over rocks, forming rapids in its path—rapids that now held me firmly in their icy grip. Seconds before, I'd been riding a log, guiding others alongside me over the rocks—until one rolled into me, knocking me into the freezing water and pinning me up to my neck. I thought I was a goner for sure . . .

As the "river boss," I knew the dangers of the springtime log drive, when crews of men would guide the felled trees along the Barrington River, down from the logging camps to my family's sawmill in Shelburne County. Jams would sometimes form along the way, with logs backing up on the bends or hitching on hidden rocks. The men often had to free up the logs. Some crews would use dynamite if the jam was too tight, but we had some pretty good drivers who could oust them with their peaveys alone: I was one of them. Displacing the logs from a jam was a dangerous job. After dislodging the ones causing the obstruction, the whole works would start moving—with you on it! It was easy to fall in or for your legs to get trapped. We all had to look out for each other on the river drives. I had to rescue plenty of fellas from the water, but

luckily that day one of them was looking out for me. Seeing me in trouble, he ferried a log across the river, rolled away the one that had me trapped and pulled me out. We had a solid crew, and our strong sense of camaraderie saved many lives.

INTO THE WOODS

My great-grandfather started our sawmill in 1883, and five generations of the family have been involved in the timber trade since. I've been at it myself for a long time, working in all areas of the business, from logging to river driving and sawing the logs at the mill, so I know my wood. Our 5,000 acres of land is covered with spruce, pine, hemlock, and oak, and our timber has mainly been used for building fishing boats.

I first went into the forest to help fell trees as a twelve-year-old. Most logging took place in winter, when there was snow on the ground. We slept in a big tent in the woods, and cooked and ate our meals in another.

Waking up for breakfast at 6 a.m., we'd be greeted by a large pot of oatmeal or cornmeal already cooking on the stove. We'd dip our bowl in, add a spoonful of molasses or sugar, and eat our fill around the fire before heading into the forest with our crosscut saws and axes to start felling. Sometimes work would be in pairs, the fella with me notching the trees and driving the wedges in before I'd start sawing, and at other times it was a solo job. At 10 a.m. we'd stop for a snack of bread, spread with molasses, and tea—there was no fresh milk or cream, so canned had to suffice. Again at noon we'd have the same, then fell trees all afternoon, finally finishing at around 6 p.m.

Food at camp was pretty good, with hearty meals of salted foods, or corned beef and pork, served with vegetables and potatoes. After dinner, there was always something to do, from mending our shoes, pike poles, or peaveys, to telling yarns. Sometimes one of the crew would play a song on their mouth organ or fiddle to lift our spirits, and we'd all sing along.

Aged fourteen, I went on the first of many spring drives,

ABOVE: Stanley and a fellow "river hog" working on the Clyde River log drive, 1932. **RIGHT:** Stanley and the crew keep the logs moving at Chrissy's Falls, where logs from the Barrington River drive passed through, 1957.

51

helping to guide the cut logs down the Barrington to the family sawmill. In my younger years, I was pretty good at being a driver—I could go most days on a log, even riding them through the rapids. You needed good balance for that. Still, it could be very wet work— we'd camp in tents along the way and all went to sleep every night in damp clothes. I remember my boss telling us not to dry them off too much at the end of each day or we'd catch a cold. Maybe he was right, because somehow we never got ill, despite our soaking socks doubling up as pillows!

Of course, there were wild animals out in the woods. One night, a black bear wandered into our camp and spooked our horse, which bolted for home, before we chased him off with our peaveys. The raccoons were more troublesome.

Stanley Scott at the Barrington River log drive, 1956.

They're pretty smart but pesky too, and we'd often find them unscrewing the lids and dipping their paws into our jars of peanut butter.

A LUMBERJACK LEGACY

Some crews used horses to pull the chopped logs on sleds to the river, but we always used a pair of oxen. Using either method was better for the forest than today's modern machinery, which can wreck the land if you don't manage it properly. I remember the first time my uncle brought home a powered chainsaw. My father couldn't get to grips with it, and thought it was dirty and loud, so he ended up throwing it into the swamp! I fished it out, cleaned it up, and repaired it, and slowly we all learned to use them.

My later years were spent driving skidders (heavy vehicles used to carry the wood to the river bank) and logging trucks, which eventually replaced the long river drives, transporting timber to the mill. I was a licensed guide for a while, too. I worked with a naturalist who wrote for *Rod & Gun* magazine,

which was about the outdoor life in Canada—I believe some of his stories about our local deer inspired the classic Disney movie *Bambi*. So my claim to fame is that I knew Bambi! I also competed in lumberjack sports—my favorites being log rolling and canoe racing. My nephew Darren has carried on the family tradition, becoming a seven-time world champion log roller and running the Wild Axe Lumberjack AXEperience, which offers visitors a chance to be a lumberjack for the day.

Our family has an eighty-year-old logging camp, which we still use today, and I like to head over there for some quiet time with my dog Billy, a Nova Scotia Duck Tolling Retriever. I've had lots of interesting and exciting experiences, and I've loved living the life of a lumberjack. There's no doubt it's hard work, but it's healthy work, too, and at eighty-eight, I still like to get out and spend time in the forest or work in the sawing mill.

We've always taken great care of our woods and still do, which is why we're able to make a good living over 130 years since we first logged our land. I hope that's the way things will continue for years and generations to come.

Loggers sometimes relied on draft animals, such as the horses shown here, to transport logs.

WWII LUMBERJILLS: THE FORGOTTEN ARMY

Not all World War II heroes fought on the frontline. In Great Britain, a hidden troop of women were waging their own daily battle in the forests, armed with axes and crosscut saws

Many valiant army divisions are remembered for the part they played in the Second World War, but there's one unit that slipped under the radar: the Women's Timber Corp (WTC). This forestry branch of the British Women's Land Army fulfilled a critical role during World War II, yet until recently its contribution to the war effort has gone largely unnoticed.

Nicknamed the forgotten army, it consisted of 15,000 to 18,000 lumberjills who responded to the 1941 call from Ernest Bevin, the UK's Minister for Labour and National Service, for women volunteers: "One million wives were wanted for war work; inconvenience would have to be suffered and younger women would have to go where their services were required. It would be better to suffer temporarily than to be in perpetual slavery to the Nazis."

The WTC was formed in 1942, after Germany's occupation of Norway cut off the transportation of essential wood supplies. Lumber was needed throughout the war to make props for the mines, telegraph poles, ship masts, railway sleepers, ladders, paper, and even grave crosses for servicemen, and with the woodsmen away fighting, it was down to women to fill their boots.

LIFE IN CAMP

Around 4,000 WTC members were deployed around the British Isles, with many working in the south of England and throughout the isolated Highlands of Scotland. Each volunteer spent two weeks at a training camp, where they were handed an ax and taught the essential skills for tree felling, snedding (removing the branches from felled trees), and loading logs onto tractors and trucks. They also learned to use a crosscut and bowman's saw, levers, cant hooks, and other vital tools of the trade.

But nothing could prepare them for the spartan living conditions of the logging camps. Packed into communal—often freezing—wooden huts, running hot water was rare, with often the only heat coming from a cast-iron stove in the dining hall. Underpaid, and with most of their wages going on bed and board, it was the friendship and support of other members that helped many of the women to survive the mental and physical challenges of being a lumberjill.

FINAL SALUTE

Working from 7 a.m. until 4:30 p.m., and later in summer months, the lumberjills did dangerous and arduous work fell-

A lumberjill working for the Women's Timber Corps carries a log on her shoulder.

ing trees by hand, while teamsters worked with Clydesdale, Belgian, and Highland Garron horses, which were used to drag the logs from the forest. Others sawed timber or drove the tractors and trucks. Working in all weathers, it was the WTC teams that helped to keep many of Britain's industries alive.

After the war ended, the WTC was disbanded in 1946, when each member handed back their uniform and received a

INTO THE WOODS

The Women's Forestry Corps was set up in 1916 during World War I, and later became part of the Women's Land Army. By 1918, up to 3,000 women were working as foresters, producing timber for the war effort. The Women's Land Army was disbanded in 1919, reforming in 1939 for World War II.

letter from Queen Elizabeth, the Queen Mother. This acknowledgment aside, these committed members drew little praise or attention for their sacrifice and efforts, until a monument was finally erected in their memory in 2007. The dedicated memorial statue, entitled *Salute*, now stands in the Queen Elizabeth Forest Park near Aberfoyle in Scotland, in honor of every lumberjill who rose to the challenge, picked up an ax, and helped to win the war.

Members of the WTC take a break from logging.

Two lumberjills use a crosscut saw to fell a tree.

LUMBERJILL TALES
Former WTC members share their memories at the unveiling of the Memorial Statue.

CHRIS FORRESTER
"We had no mechanical machinery to use; everything was done by hand. We chopped down trees with axes and crosscut saws, cut the timber into lengths, then loaded it onto tractors and trucks to be taken to the railway station."

ELIZABETH MURRAY
"I signed up in 1942 when I was seventeen. I was at a camp in Buchan near Dumfries. There were four, huts and we were lucky to have showers and running water. There was great comradeship among the girls. I don't think you get that same level of contact today using machines, but we used to really admire the trees we were felling. They were beauties."

MARGARET GRANT
"We went out every day. For the first three months you just switch off: You're sore, hungry, and tired. Then one glorious morning, you wake up to find you're a big, hulking brute and 146 pounds (66 kg) of muscle—and life is lovely! I worked a tractor, used the big saw in the mill, worked a horse, rafted timber. It was great fun. Not that I was ever weak, but it strengthened me a lot. It was lovely to work in the forest."

MARGARET KERR
"There was lots of good company and fun to be had. We were well fed, but winter was bitterly cold. The cutlery was so icy we couldn't hold it, so we would dunk the handles in our tea. One night, one of the girls woke up to find snow inside her pillow."

RITA ROBERTSON
"I was actually the replacement for a woman who was sadly killed by a tree that had fallen. I spent most of my time in the WTC on my knees, felling trees."

TIBBY SCOTLAND
"I was a teenager when I was in the WTC, and life was good. Girls coming in from offices had never worked like that before, and it was wonderful being alongside them. It was hard work, and we weren't appreciated at all at the time, so it's nice to be recognized now. We weren't fighting soldiers, but we were bringing trees down."

POETIC JUSTICE

Two poems featured in *Meet The Members: A Record Of The Women's Land Army*, 1945, capture the experience of the WWII lumberjills.

FORESTERS

They're tramping through the forest
They're trudging through the mire
They're brushing past the undergrowth
They have but one desire
Their greatest thought, their highest aim
To see in Britain, Peace again
They have no tanks or rifles
They have no stripes or drill
They have no ships or aeroplanes
But Britain needs them still
They're fighting hard with ax and saw
They're Britain's "Women's Timber Corps"
They're proud of their profession
Bad weather does not count
They bring the tall trees crashing down
The piles of pit props mount
They're doing their bit to win the war
This almost unknown "Timber Corps"
—*J. I. Melvin*

THE OTHER WAY

There is a land, or so I'm told,
Where timber girls ne'er feel the cold
Where trees come down all sned and peeled
And there's no need an ax to wield
The transport's never broken down
And Jill's go every night to town
How different here in snow and sleet
Shivering with wet and frozen feet
But wait, the sun's come out at last
And summer's here and winter's past
The lumberjills work all the day
Who'd have it round that other way?
—*Hilton Wood*

THE WTC UNIFORM

On arrival to training, each new recruit would be allocated the following:

- 2 green jerseys
- 2 pairs of riding breeches
- 2 overall coats
- 2 pairs of dungarees
- 6 pairs of woolen knee socks
- 3 beige knitted shirts
- 1 pair boots
- 1 pair of brown shoes
- 1 pair of gumboots or boots with leggings
- 1 green beret
- 1 melton overcoat
- 1 oilskin or Mackintosh
- 2 towels
- 1 green armlet and a metal badge
- 1 Bakelite hat badge

A statue commemorates the Women's Timber Corps in Aberfoyle, Scotland.

HOW TO

BE KING OF THE LUMBERJILLS

Becoming a champion lumberjack or Jill isn't just about training and skill—you need to be mentally prepared, too. World champion lumberjill Martha King shares some of the secrets of her success

"When I picked up an ax at my first timbersports competition, people didn't expect too much from someone who looked like me," says lumberjill Martha King. "For me to discover I had the timing and technique to best other competitors, including some of the guys, was so good. I felt like I'd found my place."

People now know that they underestimate Martha at their peril. She's the current world champion lumberjill, women's US Stihl champion, world underhand champion, world singlebuck champion, and world record holder in two underhand chop events. In other words, she's the fastest female woodchopper in the world.

Martha's first taste of these competitive sports came while she was studying animal sciences at The Pennsylvania State University in 2007. Following in her father's footsteps, she joined the college team and was soon winning competitions. Showing an early flair for the underhand chop, her favorite event, she also excelled in sawing, ax throwing, pole climbing, and chainsaw disciplines. "I took to timbersports like a fish to water," she says.

Martha's been around trees all her life and when she's not traveling the world and breaking records she works for her parents' tree

service company in Chadds Ford, Pennsylvania, running chainsaws, pruning and felling trees, dragging brush, and operating heavy equipment. She also spent five years working at a speciality hardwood lumber company sourcing and processing exotic woods for iconic luthiers (guitar makers) like Martin, Fender, and Gibson.

"I grew up watching my father, Robert, apply a range of forestry practices in his professional career, and on our own property," she says. "I love my parents, and I wanted to do everything my dad did—but better!"

While her family has always supported her dream to be a lumberjill, she's faced criticism from those who believe a woman's place isn't standing on a foot-thick block of pine. "I've had women saying 'girls should be girls' or telling me I should get a proper career, but I love what I do. I get to travel, meet incredible people, and I have a great platform to inspire others."

When old-school male competitors have expressed doubts about women woodchopping, Martha finds the most effective

Martha King competes in the ax-throwing event at the World Lumberjack Championships 2018 in Wisconsin.

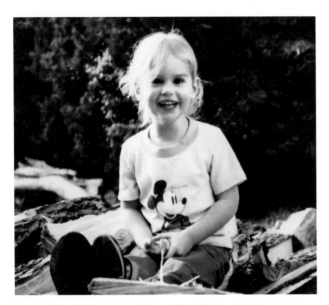

ABOVE: Martha's been around trees all her life—her family runs a tree service company. OPPOSITE: Martha is the current singlebuck world champion.

answer is a swing of her ax—not aimed at the naysayer in question (tempting), but smashing a block and busting another world record. "If someone says women don't belong in timbersports, that's when my tenacity kicks in, and I go out and cut as hard as I can," says Martha.

In 2019, that tenacity saw Martha chop and saw her way to the top of the tree in her best season yet. After winning the US Stihl Timbersports Championship, a week later she was crowned world champion lumberjill at the Lumberjack World Championships in Wisconsin, one of the sport's most prestigious competitions, where she also became the underhand chop and singlebuck world champion. She now has the Sydney Royal Easter Show in her sights, and the Australian underhand title she's yet to win. "I'm excited about what's ahead," says Martha. "I want to be a good example to people who think 'I can't do that, because I'm too this, or not enough of that.' I want to say if you're passionate about something, dedicate yourself to it, work hard, be the best you can be: there are no limits."

Martha shares some of her motivational mantras:

GARBAGE IN, GARBAGE OUT

"There's a Cherokee legend that says we have two wolves fighting inside us—two inner voices—one is darkness and despair and the other is light and hope. The wolf that wins the fight will be the one you feed. Don't listen to your inner voice that is self-critical and beats you up—feed the right beast, the one that inspires you to keep going, stay positive, and be better."

DO THE BEST YOU CAN WITH WHAT YOU HAVE

"Remember, you're the only person who's equipped to be you. And you're responsible for living your life, so don't waste time comparing yourself to others. They are who they are, and you are who you are. Focus on becoming the best person you can be and embracing your best self. Be unashamedly you. Anxiety and feelings of inadequacy will try and creep in—don't let them."

HAVE AN ATTITUDE OF GRATITUDE

"I've worked hard, but I'm not here on my own merit. I've had so many people help me along the way. I can never thank my parents enough, or the university professors who believed in me. I also owe so much to timbersports pros Laurence O'Toole and Mike Eash, who've been so supportive with my training. They broke me down and built me back up better."

MAKE TIME TO BE KIND

"No matter how long, or how hard, your day has been, don't take it out on others. Try a change of perspective. You never know what kind of day someone else might be having, and yours might be the only act of kindness they encounter. Even if it's just asking how the person at the checkout is doing, take time to engage in some meaningful conversation."

YOU'RE NEVER TOO YOUNG TO TEACH

"Sometimes I help to train timbersports students and it might be their first time lifting an ax, but they'll often say or do something that'll make me think differently about how I do things. Everyone has something to contribute, so always keep your eyes, ears, and mind open."

DIARY OF A LUMBERJILL

Here's how the woodchopping champion spends her day.

6:30 A.M.

"I wish I could say that when I wake up in the morning, I crank out a workout, meditate, and linger over breakfast, but I work my body hard, so between tree work and lumberjack training, I need all the sleep I can get! I push my snooze to the limit, do a few stretches, then get dressed, make breakfast, and pack up my lunch. I don't like to eat too soon after waking up, so I take my breakfast along as well."

7:00 A.M.

"I walk to work, as my parent's tree business isn't far. Each morning we're given the job scope for that day, anything from light pruning to removing trees with a crane. I'm usually paired with my little brother, Robbie, who is a very talented climber. It can be challenging and physically draining, but I love working with my hands on something tangible. It gives me an immediate sense of satisfaction."

12:00 P.M.

"When it comes to nutrition, I rely on my body to tell me what it needs. Rather than stop for lunch, I tend to snack and hydrate throughout the day, enjoying first and second breakfasts—maybe an English muffin sandwich, fried chicken, salmon and rice, or a fruit smoothie. On an average work day, I walk 8 miles [12.9 km], running saws and dragging brush. It's a great, full-body workout, so I can pretty much eat what I want!"

4:00 P.M.

"We usually finish work between 3:00–4:00 p.m., but sometimes later in summer. Some days I rush to set up an underhand block in the fading light and chop (very carefully!) in the lights of my dad's log truck. When I have more time, I dedicate three hours to setting up, training, studying videos, and adjusting my technique. My friend and mentor, Mike Eash, often trains with me, so it can become a bit of a social event, too."

9:00 P.M.

"My training area is at my parent's property (where the wood stash is!), so I stop in at the house after my session. My mother, Katharine, often has a plate of food ready for me, and we share news from our day. After dinner, my dad will look over my shoulder at my training videos and tell me that he is faster and more precise, as I roll my eyes and laugh! Although by now it's late, I still have a garden to weed, vegetables to pick, and a house to clean . . . but sometimes I scrap all that to take an evening hike under the stars."

11:30 P.M.

"If I'm getting up early the next morning to travel to a competition, I'll make sure I have all my gear packed and loaded, Tetris-style, in the truck. And snacks! Lots of snacks! I take a shower, which feels like a luxury after a long day cutting trees, and to help my mind slow down, I'll read or listen to a Christian podcast. I dedicate a lot of time to woodchopping, which is why I've been successful, but it's important to make time for other pursuits, which add to the fullness of life."

CHOP! CHOP!
Martha's top tips for wielding an ax like a champ . . .

"The underhand chop was the first discipline I tried at university. Some people shy away from it as it looks dangerous, but when I picked up the ax for the first time, it felt so natural. There was a bit of trepidation, as I was swinging a heavy, super-sharp object between my feet, but once I got the hang of it, it was just love.

Technique matters more than size: I'm 5 feet, 8 inches (1.7 m) and weigh 130 pounds (59 kg), so I'm tall but not a giant human. Chopping is all about how the ax meets the log, and balance and timing are key. If the ax is off-center, and your body weight is unevenly distributed, the ax will not strike the log at the right angle. This will affect how the block 'opens up,' and ultimately, the length of time it will take you to sever it. If you bring your hands together too soon at the top of your swing, the ax will be harder to control. Keep the ax in front of you as you begin your swing, keep your arms straight, and pull it into the wood. The ax naturally wants to follow the arc into the block, but a tense mind and body will complicate this simple act. Believe me, working to get this right has been quite the pursuit! I use every bit of my body and height, putting my hands together and sinking into my swing at just the right time, bringing the ax head with explosive power into the block. People think it's just wood chopping, but it's actually quite an art form."

OPPOSITE: Martha hangs out in the woods near her family home in Pennsylvania. **BELOW:** Martha competes at the annual World Lumberjack Championships in Wisconsin, 2018.
RIGHT: Martha wins the 2019 Stihl Timbersports US Women's Division Championship.

LIGHTS! CAMERA! AX-TION!

Loggers—and the tools of their trade—have starred in a rich mix of movies,
from critically acclaimed film noir, to chronically bad schlock horror. Here are five to watch
(not necessarily alone in a cabin in the woods)

THE ONE WITH THE CHAINSAW: *EVIL DEAD II*

Expensive, loud, and heavy, a chainsaw isn't the obvious choice for a murder weapon. Yet since the late 1960s, it's been the torture tool of choice for many a filmmaker, roaring through flicks from Tobe Hooper's *The Texas Chainsaw Massacre* to Brian De Palma's *Scarface*. But without a doubt, the award for Unlikeliest Use of a Chainsaw goes to Sam Raimi's 1987 comedy horror, *Evil Dead II*.

After heading to an abandoned cabin in the woods for a romantic weekend with his girlfriend, Ash Williams (Bruce Campbell) unwittingly plays cantations from the *Necronomicon Ex-Mortis* (*The Book of the Dead*), unleashing a malevolent demon—and some notoriously slick camerawork—as it whips through the forest.

A gore-fest of decapitation and chaos ensues, ramping up to a bloody crescendo which sees Ash chopping off his own possessed right hand, and strapping a customized chainsaw to the stump, before uttering the immortal line: "Groovy!" Meanwhile, the "evil hand" is subdued beneath a bucket, weighed down with a copy of Ernest Hemingway's *A Farewell to Arms*, and a heavy dose of the black humor that made the movie a cult classic.

Ash wields his groovy chainsaw hand in *Evil Dead II*.

"Here's Johnny!" *The Shining*'s iconic ax scene is one of the scariest movie moments of all time.

THE ONE WITH THE AX: *THE SHINING*

A snowbound hotel, a sinister maze, a manically cycling five-year-old, and an increasingly unhinged husband. No, this isn't a movie homage to homeschooling, nor is it a scenario that screams: "Happy vacay!" But as we discover by the end of director Stanley Kubrick's cinematic masterpiece *The Shining*, actress Shelley Duvall—who embraces the challenges that come with staying in Colorado's remote Overlook Hotel all winter—is nothing if not game. Her perseverance filming the infamous baseball bat scene 127 times before Kubrick was happy, setting a Guinness World Record for movie takes in the process, deserves at least a gold star.

Before the final credits roll on the 1980 adaptation of author Stephen King's novel, Duvall—playing Wendy, the wife of aspiring-writer-come-winter-caretaker of the Overlook, Jack Torrance (Jack Nicholson)—will find herself terrorized behind one of the most famous doors in movie history. (In fact, she would find herself behind sixty of them, the number demolished before Kubrick approved the take.) The iconic scene where a deranged Jack finally bursts through with an ax and greets his hysterical wife with a sinister "Here's Johnny!" is considered one of the scariest movie moments of all time, while for Duvall, the entire filming experience was sheer . . . murder.

65

Howard Keel eyes up Jane Powell in woodchopping musical extravaganza, *Seven Brides for Seven Brothers*.

THE ONE WITH THE DUBIOUS WOODSMEN: *SEVEN BRIDES FOR SEVEN BROTHERS*

The eponymous brothers in this movie kidnap some local lasses to be their wives and drag them back to their farm for the winter, expecting them to cook, clean, and mend for them. If you can put aside your qualms about the premise—it's 1850s Oregon we're talking about—this bouncy musical about a family gang of lovelorn backwoodsmen is sure to lighten the mood.

Stanley Donen's 1954 classic stars Howard Keel as rough and ready woodsman Adam Pontipee and Jane Powell as Milly, whose log-chopping skills catch his eye while he's striding around town, singing *Bless Yore Beautiful Hide*, and looking to trade his beaver pelts for a bride: Bingo!

Nominated for five Academy Awards, and winning the Oscar for Best Music Scoring of a Musical Picture, the movie's expertly choreographed set pieces, including the lumberjack-tastic barn-raising scene and *Lonesome Polecat*—which sees the siblings singing about their singledom to the steady rhythm of their axes and saws—may just win you over, too.

THE ONE WITH THE WOOD CHIPPER: *FARGO*

If you ever need to dispose of a body with minimum noise and fuss, the method used in Joel and Ethan Coen's brilliant 1996 film noir *Fargo* may not be the one for you. Turns out that running a man through a woodchipper after killing him with an ax is mighty loud and messy work, especially when it's done in a snow-covered wood. Who knew? (Hopefully nobody reading this book).

In an Oscar-winning performance, actress Frances McDormand plays pregnant police chief Marge Gunderson, who discovers the gruesome scene while investigating a triple-homicide in Minnesota. In less bloody nods to the state's logging history, *Fargo* features a giant statue of Paul Bunyan with an ax looming above a highway sign saying: "Welcome to Brainerd"—rumored to be the home of the legendary lumberjack—while the movie's criminals stay at the Blue Ox Motel.

While the Bunyan statue is no longer there, movie fans can catch him and Babe at Brainerd's Paul Bunyan Land, before recreating the woodchipper moment on a visit to the Fargo-Moorhead Visitors Center: Home to one of the most famous movie props in history, complete with a protruding leg.

THE ONE WITH THE DEMON LOGGER: *LUMBERJACK MAN*

Imagine *Friday the 13th* with a wagon of flapjacks and a pike pole, and you'll have a pretty good idea of what to expect from Josh Bear's 2015 comedy horror. All the standard slasher movie tropes are here: A group of rowdy teenagers? Check. A summer camp in the woods? Check. An undead murderer with a lust for blood? Check. Plaid shirt? Check. Check.

But what's driving this demon logger to fell teens quicker than a Stihl MS 881? According to legend, it's wronged woodsman Nehemiah Easterday's insatiable desire to finish off his flapjacks by Lent, slathered with the blood of his victims instead of syrup. Ahh, so now it makes total sense! "This camp sits on the Sinkhole of Hell," warns Dr. Peter Shirtcliff, the survivor of a previous syrup massacre, played by much-too-good-for-this-movie actor Michael Madsen. Which makes you wonder which member of the committee had the bright idea of setting up a summer camp over a festering Hadean pit, when land surveys are so readily available.

But hey, who are we to question the illogical decisions made in a teen slasher movie? Without them, there would *be* no

teen slasher movie. So on we romp, as the lumbering villain finds increasingly grizzly ways to chop down teens with his (quite expertly wielded) ax. With an appropriate soundtrack by Chainsaw, this is a fun one to watch with the lights out and a stack of pancakes. Just remember, in the words of the movie trailer: "Don't get axed!"

Don't get axed! Lumberjack Man is on the hunt for flapjacks.

CALL OF THE WILD

Lumberjacks weren't the only varmints roaming the forests of North America during the logging boom. Check out some of the animals they may have run into in the woods

MOOSE

Nothing can prepare you for the monumental beauty of a moose until you see one emerging from a stand of aspen or swimming across a rumbling river, its magnificent antlers cradling the skies above.

Like the lumberjack, these giants of North America encompass the spirit of wilderness and outdoor adventure. Found in the US and Canada, as well as parts of Europe and Asia, the moose is the largest of the deer species, growing up to 7 feet (2.1 m) at the shoulder and weighing up to 1,800 lb, with antlers that can span 6 feet (1.8 m). Despite their size, they're fast runners, reaching speeds of 35 miles per hour (56 km/h), and excellent swimmers, known to submerge for a minute at a time.

While they're not naturally aggressive, moose will attack if they feel threatened, with bulls more feisty during the fall mating season and cows becoming protective of their calves in late spring and summer, so always keep your distance.

MOOSE MUSHING

While moose haven't been widely domesticated, Albert Vaillancourt of Chelmsford, Ontario, trained two rescued moose calves to pull a sleigh, and toured Canada with his unconventional sled team in the 1940s.

GRIZZLY BEAR

An awe-inspiring predator, the grizzly is a North American subspecies of the brown bear, which is found in Asia and Europe. Mothers with cubs aside, grizzlies are mainly solitary animals and roam widely through forests, alpine meadows, and prairies. While much of their diet consists of nuts, berries, and roots, they also eat fish and animals, including rodents and even moose.

Measuring up to 5 feet (1.5 m) at the shoulder, the bears can tower up to 9 feet (2.7 m) tall when standing on their hind legs: a sight every lumberjack working in the backcountry hoped never to see. Luckily for the loggers, while most of their work was carried out the bears would be safely ensconced in their winter dens, but once the mothers emerged with their cubs in spring, the woodsmen had to be bear aware.

While the grizzly's size and power invoked fear, it also earned the animal great respect from the indigenous peoples—some tribes believe the bear is a deity and connected to the spirit world.

SPOT THE DIFFERENCE
Grizzlies and brown bears are generally larger than black bears, have a prominent hump at the shoulder, shorter ears, a concave or "dished" facial profile, and longer, straighter claws.

WOLF

The howl of a gray wolf in the night fills some with wonder and others with woe. This powerful apex predator has always invoked extreme reactions and split opinions.

America's forests and prairies belonged to the wolves before pioneers rolled their wagons into the West and the resulting demise of their prey species—bison, deer, and elk—forced packs to target domestic animals for food. Hunted almost to extinction by the mid-1930s, wolves are now seeing a comeback in the United States, with a successful reintroduction program in Yellowstone National Park highlighting the vital role that they play in maintaining healthy ecosystems.

Also found in Canada, Europe, and Asia, gray wolves are highly social, living in packs of six to ten, led by an alpha male and female. The largest species of the dog family can stand up to 3 feet (0.9 m) tall and weigh up to 175 pounds (79 kg). While they can survive for days without making a kill, they can also wolf down a whopping 20 pounds (9 kg) of meat in one sitting.

HOWL DO YOU DO?

Each wolf has its own unique howl, used to communicate with other members of the pack and to warn other packs away from their territory. The howl can carry up to 10 miles (16 km) on open land.

BEAVER

Canoe any remote river in North America and if you're lucky, you'll hear the joyous slap of a beaver's tail. Nature's consummate lumberjacks are experts in plying their trade, gnawing through trees as deftly as a misery whip and building dams to rival any laid down by a river hog.

Found in North America, Europe, and Asia, these semiaquatic rodents are second only to South America's capybaras in size, weighing a stocky 60 pounds (27 kg). Measuring up to 39 inches (99 cm) in length, with a 12-inch (30 cm) tail, their streamlined bodies, webbed hind feet and rudderlike tail make them excellent swimmers, while thick fur protects them in icy waters. But most amazing, of course, are their teeth, which include four continuously growing, orange incisors.

BEAVERS BITE BACK

Eurasian beavers are being reintroduced to parts of the United Kingdom after they became extinct in the sixteenth century following hunting for their fur, meat, and "castoreum," a secretion used in food, perfumes, and medicine.

Beavers live in family groups inside "lodges," built from branches and mud. Inhabiting a range of freshwater habitats, including rivers and ponds, they lead the way when it comes to landscaping. Not only will their dams slow down a river's flow, they'll also create wetland habitats, allowing other species to flourish.

WHITE-TAILED DEER

These fine-looking deer (also known as the Virginia deer) are found across the Americas, as well as parts of Europe and the Caribbean. Living in brushy, forested habitats, savannahs, and agricultural landscapes, they grow to 42 inches (107 cm) at the shoulder, and weigh up to 400 pounds (181 kg).

In warmer months, they have a rich, red coat that turns grayish-brown in winter. They take their name from the white fur on the underside of their tail, which they flash when alarmed—warning predators that they've been seen—before darting for cover. They can escape at speeds of 30 miles per hour (48 km/h)and clear 30 feet (9.1 m) in a single bound.

The bucks (male deer) grow impressive antlers in the summer and fall and compete in sparring matches over territories and does (females), which give birth to one to three white-spotted fawns in spring. One of them you might know; he was the star of the Disney movie, *Bambi*.

HOW TO
SURVIVE A BEAR ATTACK

You're out in the woods when a supersized grizzly wanders your way.
Do you: a) switch your phone to selfie mode; b) go in for a bear hug; or c) wish you had paid more attention to that infamous six-minute scene in *The Revenant*? (Correct answer below)

Whilst most forays into the wilderness will be happily incident-free, it makes sense to know what to do if you encounter a 700-pound (318 kg) grizzly. Most bears will run away at the terrifying sight of a hairy, plaid-wearing human, but if you catch one by surprise—especially a mother with cubs—it could feel threatened and attack. How you react could mean the difference between walking away unscathed or being left for dead like DiCaprio (thanks, buddies).

BE BEAR AWARE
The best way to survive a bear attack is to avoid it in the first place.

- *Never* enter bear country without bear spray—and know how to use it before you set off. Bear spray has a 20-foot (6.1 m) spread at a 25-foot (7.6 m) range and is the best deterrent for a bear attack; keep it handy in a holster.

- If you're in bear territory, be loud. Sing and clap your hands so that any bears know you're nearby and can leave the area.
- Avoid walking or working alone—when it comes to bears, there's safety in numbers.
- Don't zone out on your phone or wear headphones or earbuds—if there are bears around, stay alert.
- Be mindful of blind bends on your path and approach them noisily and with caution.
- Avoid venturing into dense bush and berry patches, where bears might be feeding.
- Never approach a lone cub or place yourself between a mother bear and her cubs. If she perceives you as a threat, she could attack.
- Never feed a bear and always make sure any food or toiletries are locked away safely in bear-resistant containers; they have a great sense of smell.

SURVIVAL MODE

You've done all you can to avoid a bear, but a big mama is eyeballing you. Keeping yourself—and the bear—calm is crucial.

- Never, ever run: acting like a prey animal will activate the bear's chase reflex. Pick up any children immediately and group together.
- Quietly take up your bear spray and remove the safety lock.
- Remain still and calm, as you slowly position the spray.
- Speak to the bear in soothing, low tones to let it know you're a human.
- If the bear is stationary, move away slowly and sideways, so you can keep an eye on the bear and avoid tripping. Make yourself look bigger by moving to higher ground if you can. If the bear follows, stop and stand still.
- Do not climb a tree—both grizzly and black bears are adept climbers—and do not drop your backpack: it could provide protection for your back should you need it.
- The bear may stand on its hind legs to get a better look or smell you—this means it's curious, but not necessarily threatening.
- Woofing, yawning, salivating, growling, snapping their jaws, and laying their ears back are defensive bear behaviors. Continue to talk in low tones to try and calm the bear.
- The bear may run toward you in a bluff charge, but only use the spray if the bear approaches within 20–30 feet (6.1–9.1 m) of you, or it won't work.
- If the bear comes within range, follow the manufacturer's instructions and trigger the spray with a sustained blast to create a cloud between you, adjusting for any wind. This should stop the attack. If it continues, spray directly into the bear's face. Leave the area slowly after spraying.

NO BEAR SPRAY?

You've stayed calm and followed the rules, but a bear is about to attack and you've gone and left the bear spray in the car. Time for extreme survival mode.

Grizzly bear: If you're attacked by a grizzly bear, play dead. Lie flat on your stomach and clasp your hands behind your neck. Spread your legs to make it harder for the bear to turn you over and remain as still as you can until the bear leaves you alone. Fighting back usually increases the intensity of the attack, but if the attack persists, fight back using whatever you have to hit the bear in the face.

Black bear: If you're attacked by a black bear, do not play dead. Try to escape to a secure place like a building or car. If escape isn't possible, fight back with anything available, aiming your blows at the bear's face and muzzle.

Before entering bear country, always ask a local visitor center or backcountry office for the latest bear safety information.

> **WALK, DON'T RUN**
> Adult grizzly bears can run up to 40 miles per hour (64 km/h), so unless you're a greyhound, don't even think about outrunning a charging grizzly.

FEARSOME CRITTERS OF THE LUMBERWOODS

We're not talking bears or bobcats. We're talking gumberoos, squonks, and snoligosters. Be very afraid!

Maybe it's about living in a remote part of the world, or spending too much time in a forest. Perhaps it's a sign of an overactive imagination, or just a symptom of drinking too much moonshine. Whatever the reason, the world's wildest regions often give rise to myths of mysterious beasts—sometimes scary (Mothman, Wendigo), often hairy (Sasquatch, Bigfoot), and always with no hard evidence at all that they exist.

While lumberjacks came into contact with plenty of real-life beasts that could attack them (hello, Mr. Grizzly), it was the tall tales told around the campfire that really put the wind up the woodsmen. The critters that filled the shanty boys' yarns made a bear encounter sound like a picnic. Loggers would move from camp to camp, sharing their stories of fantastic beasts of the forest. While some were clearly invented for scares, others manifested to make sense of the lumberjacks' world, adding humor and intrigue to the serious, sad, or mundane. Here are a few to watch out for next time you go down to the woods.

THE GUMBEROO

If you find yourself face-to-face with this hairless beast, remember that fire is your friend. While its thick, leathery skin renders it nearly indestructible, a flame will see it conveniently swell up and spontaneously—and loudly—explode.

THE SNOLIGOSTER

You'll find this crocodilian creature lurking in the swamps around Lake Okeechobee in Florida. It loves meat, tossing its victims onto the sharp spike on its back with a flick of its tail, where they'll stay until supper, when it grinds them up in a hole before inhaling or drinking them down.

THE HUGAG

Blessed with stamina to outwalk any hunters on its trail, this prehistoric moose-like beast can be found wandering America's lake states and Canada's Hudson Bay. It grazes on trees with its oversize lip and leans against them to sleep. Why? Its stiff, jointless legs render it unable to lie down.

THE HODAG

Hailing from Rhinelander, Wisconsin, this ugly critter has bulging eyes and a spiny back and has been known to sob loudly about its appearance. Luckily, a fear of citrus fruits means you can see it off with a lemon.

THE SQUONK

Home for this shy, morose monster is the hemlock forests of Pennsylvania, where it roams at dusk, eager to stay out of sight. Covered with lumpy warts and moles, it likes a good cry and is prone to dissolve in the flood of its own tears when looked upon, cornered, or trapped.

THE WHIRLING WHIMPUS

If you're wandering the trails of Tennessee, watch out. This bloodthirsty, gorilla-shaped being catches its prey (you) by whirling around so speedily that it becomes invisible, while omitting a loud droning noise. On investigating, you'll be pulverized by its rotating paddle-arms and licked up for its deliciously sticky supper. Bon appétit.

THE GUMBEROO

THE HODAG

THE SNOLIGOSTER

THE SQUONK

THE HUGAG

THE WHIRLING WHIMPUS

HOW TO
BE A HIGH CLIMBER

Who better than world champion tree climber Stirling Hart to inspire you to climb to new heights?

Lumberjackin' wasn't all about chopping and sawing with your feet planted firmly on the ground. "High climbers" or "tree toppers" would use hooks and ropes to climb trees, with some species standing up to 300 feet (91 m) high, sawing off tree tops before the fallers went to work. After dinner, the toppers would compete, challenging each other to see who could climb faster or higher—the inspiration for today's competitions.

Contemporary arborists and forestry workers still have a head for heights, chopping the tops off trees to reduce the risk of them falling in high winds, and spending up to eight hours off the ground, swinging from tree to tree in true Tarzan style. When he's not smashing world records or competing in championships across the globe, Canadian lumberjack and arborist Stirling Hart runs a forestry company, thinning trees for growth and fire protection around British Columbia.

A third-generation lumberjack—his family owned a sawmill, and both his grandfather and father were loggers and accomplished competitors—Stirling had his first rope, belt, and spurs (climbing spikes) aged four, and started scaling up to around 10-foot (3 m) trees. Fast-forward to 2010 and he claimed his first world record as a tree climber, racing up and down a 100-foot (30 m) tree in just 23.3 seconds.

In 2013, he broke the 90-foot (27 m) climbing world record with 18.3 seconds, and the 80-foot (24 m) world record with 17.81 seconds. Switching to chopping and sawing competitions in 2014, Stirling scooped further honors, before winning the Stihl Timbersports Champions Trophy in 2018, completing all four disciplines—stock saw, underhand chop, single buck, and standing block chop—in under 65 seconds to win the title.

"Working in the forest is essentially what won me the competitions," says Stirling, who was born near Vancouver and now lives in Squamish, where he also performs in a local lumberjack show. "Climbing 270-foot (83 m) Douglas firs for a living is the best training and conditioning I could have. Being a lumberjack has allowed me to travel all over the world and meet amazing people. It's totally shaped my life."

The world's fastest tree climbers can race up and down poles in seconds.

THE COMPETITION

Competitors race head-to-head up and down twin cedar poles of various heights, aiming for the fastest time. Starting with one foot on the ground and one beneath the orange marker line, on the starting signal they use climbing spurs and steel-core climbing ropes to scale the poles up to the height mark. They then quickly descend, touching the pole a specified number of times with their feet on the way down. In some countries, competitors belay back down the pole, rather than climbing.

Stirling's top tree-climbing tips will take you straight to the top:

SET YOUR GOALS

"You need to have a goal in mind, because training is hard and you're going to find any excuse not to do it! Having a goal is the carrot you need to keep you motivated and focused—set yours as high as the trees you want to climb."

LISTEN TO YOUR BODY

"A lot of people will run or weightlift as much as they can, but that doesn't always get the best results. In the run-up to a competition in July, I'll ramp up my training in February, go hard in April and May with gym work and sprinting, then wind down to give myself the chance to recover."

ACCEPT THE PAIN

"Descending is far more dangerous than climbing up a tree, and at times I've hurt myself pretty badly. I've broken feet, twisted ankles, sprained knees, torn hip ligaments, displaced my pelvis, dislocated shoulders, lost skin on my forearms and knuckles, and had a *lot* of splinters. I also have a 5-inch (13 cm) scar on my right cheek from when an ax fell out of a tree, narrowly missing my eye—it's become my trademark! But when you do well, it's worth it—the pain is part of the passion."

BUILD ON EXPERIENCE

"When I was younger, I'd get nervous during a competition and think about screwing up. Now I know that as I put my all into training, I can only do my best. A little bit of adrenaline can help drive your performance, but try and find a way to keep your nerves in check. The more experience you have climbing, the more you'll increase in confidence and trust in your abilities."

EAT FOR SPEED

"To be a great climber, you need to have explosive speed rather than weight, so clean food is what you need. When I was competing in tree climbing, I'd eat smaller meals, as it's not great to have a lot of weight on your knees when you're coming down the pole. My diet consisted of lean meat, whole foods, eggs, and lots of vegetables. I'd drink lots of water, and supplement with protein, green powders, and amino acids."

STAY POSITIVE

"If you want to do well, you'll need to work on training your mind as well as your body. Losing is tough for everybody, but it's how you handle it that matters. Coming second in a competition actually inspired me to do better next time. Finding the motivation to stay on top is often the hardest part of winning."

RIGHT: Stirling Hart set the current springboard world record with a time of 35.67 seconds at the 2016 Stihl World Championships.
LEFT: Canadian Champion Hart competes in the single buck discipline at The Stihl Timbersports Champions Trophy, 2018.

PRETTY IN INK

What better way to adorn those fine, woodchopping arms than with some striking body art? From retro Jacks and Jills to fierce forest beasts, the tattoo options for pledging your lumberjack allegiance are endless. Here's some inspiration if you're thinking about getting one of your own

ICE AGE LUMBERJACK

The oldest tattoos found on a person covered the frozen body of Ötzi the Iceman, who was discovered buried under glacier ice in Italy's South Tyrol in 1991. Scientifically dated to 3250 BCE,

Ötzi had sixty-one tattoos in the form of lines and crosses, made by rubbing charcoal into fine cuts in his skin. The Copper Age mummy was found with a dagger, a bow—and an ax.

THE BIG SPRING DRIVE

The end of winter and melting snow signaled the start of the most dramatic—and dangerous—event of the year: the log drive

After a busy winter of chopping and sawing in the woods, the spring melt announced it was time for one of the most thrilling activities in the lumber calendar. Before logging roads and railways were constructed, millions of felled logs were floated down the rivers to the sawmills. Depending on the amount of timber and the river's length and layout, the journey could take days, weeks, or months, with crews camping along the way, as they guided the logs to their destination.

Known as log drivers, river jacks, or river pigs, the men who managed the drive were brave, hardy, agile, and adept at keeping the timber moving through the raging rapids and around treacherous bends. Often riding the logs, with spiked—or calked—boots to help secure their footing, they used peaveys to free up stuck logs and clear jams. Falling off could be fatal, with icy waters, hidden rocks, and heavy trunks claiming many drivers who risked their lives working some of the world's mightiest rivers.

SKILLED CREW

With so much hanging on a safe and successful drive, good management was essential. Experienced members would go ahead to clear potential sticking points on the river, then the main body of the crew traveled with the logs, keeping them moving and quickly breaking up any jams. Younger, greener men followed toward the back in the "rear crew," ensuring no logs were left behind, and freeing any strays with their pike poles.

On stretches of river lacking a strong current or lakes, the logs would be gathered together in a "boom"—a floating log chain or barrier—and winched along by a "bateau", or small boat. Bateaux were also used to carry men out to reach stuck timber, but drivers would often leap on a log and simply ride it across the river to free up a jam, showing balance and skill.

A HERO'S WELCOME

The boss or foreman called the shots, employed for his knowledge of the river and ability to keep a crew of rowdy lumberjacks in check, both on the river and in camp each night. The spring drive would only start when he deemed the river ready, with a few sticks of strategically placed dynamite sometimes used to help break up thawing ice and set the logs on their way. A wooden raft, known as a wannigan, followed the drive, carrying tents, bedrolls, and the

HIGH & DRY

This phrase was first used to describe logs that became stuck on a drive where the flow of a river wasn't high enough to carry them all the way to the mill. This sometimes meant waiting until the following spring to get them moving again.

At this 1937 log drive, about 13 million feet (3,900 m) of logs and 30,000 cords of pulpwood were transported down the Little Fork River in Koochiching County, Minnesota.

THE LOG DRIVER'S WALTZ

The classic Canadian folk song "The Log Driver's Waltz," written by singer and songwriter Wade Hemsworth in the 1950s, champions the men's skills on both the river and dance floor, as they twirl and birl their way into the hearts of locals. It was made into a brilliantly buoyant animated short of the same name in 1979.

If you ask any girl from
the parish around
What pleases her most from
her head to her toes
She'll say, I'm not sure that
it's business of yours
But I do like to waltz with a log driver

[Chorus]
For he goes birling down and
down white water
That's where the log driver
learns to step lightly
Yes, birling down and down
white water
The log driver's waltz
pleases girls completely

When the drive's nearly over
I like to go down
And watch all the lads as
they work on the river
I know that come evening
they'll be in the town
And we all like to waltz
with the log driver

[Repeat chorus]

To please both my parents,
I've had to give way
And dance with the doctors and
merchants and lawyers
Their manners are fine,
but their feet are of clay
And there's none with the
style of my log driver

[Repeat chorus]

Now I've had my chances
with all sorts of men
But none as so fine as
my lad on the river
So when the drive's over,
if he asks me again
I think I will marry my log driver

[Repeat chorus]

Birling down and down white water
The log driver's waltz
pleases girls completely

---

tent, played music, told yarns, and dried wet clothes around the fire. If they camped near a town or village, sometimes they'd show off their log rolling or "birling" skills in an effort to impress the locals, too. And when the men and the logs finally made it to their final destination, there were celebrations all round. After braving the wildest of white water and risking all for the big drive, none were more deserving of a hero's welcome.

THE WORLD'S BIGGEST JAMS

Despite the skill and vigilance of the crew, log jams still occurred, with hotspots being the twists and turns of the river, sandbars, deadheads, and rapids. Here are a few of the largest recorded pile-ups which drew crowds from miles around to witness the never-ending rivers of logs.

ST. CROIX RIVER, MINNESOTA/ WISCONSIN, 1886

Someone was likely sent to the naughty step for allowing this monumental jam to back up for a whopping five miles at the river's Dalles gorge, near Taylors Falls, on the Minnesota–Wisconsin border. An estimated 50 million board feet of white pine clogged the river for six weeks, with 400 men, two steamboats, horse teams, and a 24-pound (11 kg) dynamite bomb finally managing to clear the "jammedest jam," as it was named by a local news reporter.

GRAND RIVER, MICHIGAN, 1883

When heavy rains overwhelmed the lumbering booms on West Michigan's Grand River, a huge jam threatened to decimate the state's logging industry. Canadian marine engineer John Walsh, who only had one arm, was heralded for breaking the congestion and averting disaster, preventing 37

---

drivers' gear, along with the cook, their helper, a stove and food provisions for the crew. After ten hours of arduous river work, and with the logs safely corralled for the night in booms on the river, the men sat down to a hearty meal in the dining million tons of logs floating into Lake Michigan and being lost. According to reports, the number of logs stacked up in "The Great Log Jam of 1883" would have stretched almost 28,000 miles (45,061 km) if laid end-to-end, enough to encircle the Earth once, with timber to spare.

WISCONSIN RIVER, 1884

Men worked for a month trying to clear this enormous log jam at Grandfather Falls, without success. The river drivers were moving around one million board feet of pine and while two-thirds made it over the falls in high water, around 32 million board feet were left high and dry. Eventually jam-breaker extraordinaire Jim Crane sent the logs on their way, working for two weeks with dynamite to free the wood.

DRIVERS ON FILM

For a fascinating glimpse into the life of a log driver, you can't beat the beautiful short film *La Drave (Log Drive)* by director Raymond Garceau. Produced by the National Film Board of Canada, the 1957 documentary features jaunty lumberjack shanties from Wade Hemsworth and follows the big spring drive along the river to a "hungry timber mill" in Québec.

The St. Croix River log jam became a tourist attraction. Thousands of visitors traveled to Taylors Falls, Minnesota, to see the piled-up logs.

LOG ROLL LIKE A PRO

Follow these top tips from six-time world champion Shana Verstegen
and you'll discover log rolling is easy as, er, falling off a log

A group of lumberjacks prepare for the log drive near Littlefork, Minnesota, 1937.

"River pigs"—the men who managed the drive—fight the foam of the Cleanwater River to move a white pine log, Idaho, 1961.

The sport of log rolling originated in the spring river drives of the late 1800s, when "log drivers" or "river pigs" guided and rode logs from the forest logging sites down the river to the lumber mill. Hard and perilous work, it brought regular soakings in icy cold water and the risk of being crushed in log jams, or even drowning.

The safe arrival of the logs and crew was always a cause for celebration, with locals coming out to meet the men to congratulate them on a drive well run. As the stars of the show, the lumberjacks would entertain their adoring audience with daring feats that displayed their logging skills, strength, and bravery, competing in ax throwing, chopping competitions, and, of course, log rolling. Two or three men would stand on a log and roll it out until just one was left standing, to be crowned the best "birler," or log roller.

Honoring the log drivers' legacy today, men, women, and children of all ages log roll in pools, ponds, and lakes across the world, while pro-athletes compete in national and world championships, toppling opponents and records alike.

Born and raised in Madison, Wisconsin, Shana Verstegen has won six world championships—four for log rolling and two for boom running—and is a Great Outdoor Games and Stihl Timbersports Series gold medallist. She's also the coowner of Madison Log Rolling, which runs programs for kids and adults.

"Log rolling really is a sport anyone can do," says Shana. "You don't need to be particularly athletic, you just need to put some time into practice. And unlike some of the lumberjack sports, you don't need to be big or strong—in fact, some of the best log rollers are smaller, more agile competitors."

Now it's your turn! Follow Shana's top tips and soon you'll be rolling like a champ.

1. "The hardest thing about starting to log roll is finding the right kind of log and a body of water to roll it on. The logs we use are 12–13 feet (3–4 m) long and are generally made from Canadian red cedar wood, although synthetic logs are becoming more widely available. While they're very buoyant, they're also pretty heavy and hard to transport, so it's better—and safer—to learn at a club."

2. "When you first get on a log, make sure someone is holding it steady for you. Slowly stand up and find your center of gravity. You may find it easier barefoot—once you have some experience, you can invest in spiked shoes, which help to increase traction on the log."

3. "Always look at the far end of the log. This will help you maintain your balance and condition you to look at your opponent's feet when you start to compete. If you take your eyes off the log, you'll fall in immediately—you've been warned!"

4. "When you're ready to start rolling, move your feet up and down as fast as you can, as if the log's made of hot lava. Your brain can't react fast enough to the sudden direction changes of the log, so if your feet are already moving ahead of time, you'll be better prepared to react to the log's movements."

5. "Position your feet to find your balance over the top of the log and put your outside arm in front of your body to help stay centered. If you feel you're going to fall off, shift your body weight or change your position."

6. "Now just keep marching. As you gain confidence, you can practice spinning, jerking, stopping, and changing the log's direction to topple your opponent. But at the start, if you manage to stay on the log for more than five seconds, you're already a superstar!"

ABOVE: Shana Verstegen has won six world championships, including two for boom running. **OPPOSITE:** World champion Shana teaches the art of log rolling in Madison, Wisconsin.

HOW TO SINK YOUR OPPONENT

"You need to gain control of the log at the right time to dislodge your competitor," says Shana. "Catch them off balance and they'll be susceptible to your attack. If their shoulders, hips, or feet slip out of position, that's when to make your killer move. Remember, you're on the same log, so you're connected. To stop them attacking, you need to 'lock up the log' by dipping your toes or your heels in the water—we call it boxing with your feet!"

THE COMPETITION

Two log rollers stand on the same log, at different sides of a central dividing line that they cannot cross. Competitors are not allowed to push or touch each other, but must try to knock the other into the water by rocking, spinning the log, or splashing, unbalancing their opponent before the time limit expires. To win a match, log rollers must dislodge their opponent from the log three times. Competition logs have varying diameters, with smaller logs rolling faster in the water, and competitors wear spiked shoes to help with traction on the log. But it's your resilience and determination to keep getting back up after each dipping that will really make you a champ.

THE LEGENDARY LUMBERJACK BIG JOE MUFFERAW

While the US has supersized Paul Bunyan, Canada has its own ax-wielding, river-driving hero in the form of rough 'n' ready woodsman Big Joe Mufferaw

The debate surrounding the existence of American lumberjack Paul Bunyan continues, but there's little doubt that Canada's own logging legend was based on a real-life bûcheron (woodsman).

Joe Montferrand was born in 1802, in Montreal, Québec. Strong and agile, he became known as an outstanding athlete. He also often got into fights, dishing out hidings to local troublemakers and competing in boxing matches, knocking out the Canadian champion aged just sixteen in Québec City.

Standing 6 feet, 4 inches (1.9 m) tall with blue eyes and fair hair, Montferrand loved the great outdoors. He joined the famed Hudson's Bay Company at twenty-one, working as a voyageur, a dangerous job that involved transporting pelts along Canada's rivers by canoe, to satisfy the demands of the fur trade.

SHINER SHOWDOWN

In 1827, Montferrand began working as a lumberjack and river driver on the Rivière du Nord and the Ottawa River. Never one to shy away from conflict, he became a champion for the French-Canadian lumbermen who were caught up in violent clashes with Shiners—Irish immigrants who were eager to make their fortune from logging the Ottawa Valley's "big timber."

One tale recounts how he took on a crowd of 150 Shiners who ambushed him on the bridge between Hull and Bytown (now Ottawa). Undeterred by their number, he picked up the largest Irishman by his feet and swung him around like a club, sending the leaders of the mob flying into the river, and the remainder fleeing the scene.

Later, Montferrand moved to Outaouais in western Québec, and after 1840 he worked as the foreman on log drives, until his retirement in 1857. After the death of his first wife, he married again in the spring of 1864, before passing away peacefully that October in Montreal. His son was born after his death, growing up to be as tall and strong as his father. Sir Wilfred Laurier, Canada's prime minster at the turn of the twentieth century, described Montferrand as possessing "undaunted bravery, muscular strength, thirst for danger,

A 16-foot (4.9 m) tall statue of Big Joe stands outside the Mattawa Museum in Ontario, Canada.

JOS MONTFERRAND *BÛCHERON LÉGENDAIRE*
LEGENDARY LUMBERJACK

CANADA 42

ing his name as "Muffero," "Muffera," and the version that stuck, "Mufferaw."

He was included in two books by Joan Finnegan, *Giants of the Ottawa Valley* (1981) and *Look! The Land is Growing Giants* (1983), which reaffirmed his reputation as a larger-than-life hero. Author Bernie Bedore further cemented Mufferaw's rightful place in Canadian culture in his popular book series *Tall Tales of Joe Mufferaw* (1979), *More Tall Tales of Joe Mufferaw* (1981), and *Mythical Mufferaw* (1994).

MAKING HIS MARK

Like Paul Bunyan, Big Joe is credited for influencing the landscapes where he logged, creating the Rideau Canal from the path he trod, while carrying his canoe to see his girlfriend; extinguishing a forest fire with five spitballs; and single-handedly constructing Mount St. Pat. He also left his boot prints on 8-foot-high (2 m) ceilings—one of his favorite tricks while impressing the ladies with his backflips. And just as Bunyan had Babe, Mufferaw's companion was a pet frog that was "bigger than a horse and barked like a dog."

In 1970, Big Joe made the leap from the printed page to the top of the charts, with a song by country music star Stompin' Tom Connors, which made it to number one. Entitled *Big Joe Mufferaw*, it mentions several tall tales about the lumberjack, including Lake Mississippi being formed from the giant's dripping sweat, and the time he fought twenty-nine men in the Pembroke Pub after drinking a bucket of gin, "leaving twenty-nine boot marks . . . signed with love."

Like his fellow folk hero and strongman Bunyan, Big Joe Mufferaw has left his own indelible signature stamped on North America's landscapes, history, and culture, too.

and resistance to fatigue." He also called him "the most truly Canadian of all Canadians ever known."

TALL TALES

A legend while he was alive, Montferrand's reputation continued to grow after his death, as writers attributed increasingly fantastical feats to his already impressive list of achievements. Published in 1884, his biography by Benjamin Sulte, *Histoire de Montferrand L'Athlète Canadien*, describes the woodsman as a "homme extraordinaire," who personified a historic and honorable past. His popular folklore name came from mispronunciation, with non-French speakers interpret-

LEFT: Joseph Montferrand was featured on a Canadian stamp in 1992.
OPPOSITE: These illustrations come from *Histoire de Jos. Monteferrand* (1899), a collection of stories about Big Joe Mufferaw, who was also known as Jos among French-Canadians.

JOS. MONTFERRAND

Il s'enleva d'un vigoureux coup de jarret, et marqua
les clous de sa botte sur le plafond.

Montferrand se sentit atteint derrière la tête par un coup de pierre....

POWER OF ART

The US Open Chainsaw Sculpture Championship brings together some of the world's best carvers, who spend four days transforming wood into works of art

"We like them sharp and running fast," says Steven Higgins, talking about the tools of his trade: chainsaws. But Steven doesn't use his collection of fifty saws to cut down trees—he uses them to carve intricate, award-winning artworks from wood. Raised in Northport, Washington, in the shadow of the forests of the Pacific Northwest, Steven honed his skills during a seven-year apprenticeship with a master carver, which he began aged just eleven.

By fifteen, he started competing and has been traveling the world on the carving circuit ever since. Now based in Missouri, Steven's mesmerizing "Mother Nature" sculpture scooped him the champion's title at the US Open event. "It's all about finding the beauty of the wood and then figuring out how to let the natural tones play off of each other," says Steven. "Wood carving is my natural habitat, and the chainsaw is almost an extension of my hand."

The US Open Chainsaw Sculpture Championship takes place annually at the Wisconsin Logging Museum in Eau Claire.

In the 2019 competition, Steven Higgins won first place for a piece called "Mother Nature" (left). Corey Worden came in second place for his sculpture of eagles (opposite, top row, far left), while Chris Kuehn took third place for his sculpted bear (opposite, second row). Fourth place went to Chris Wood for his wolf sculpture (opposite, bottom row, far left).

HOW TO
LIVE THE LUMBERJACK LIFESTYLE

It's not just about wearing plaid and grooming your whiskers—it's also about working hard, inner strength, and a lusty appetite for the great outdoors (OK, maybe it's a little bit about the cool shirts, too). US champion Cassidy Scheer shares his tips for living your lumberjack dreams

As the world's population becomes increasingly urbanized, spending more time indoors, stressed, and sitting at desks, the appeal of spending time in the wilderness grows. For the men and women who work in the woods or compete in logging-inspired sports, being a lumberjack or Jill offers a lifestyle that not only encompasses the trademark look of the logger, but also offers a deep connection to the great outdoors.

Nobody is living this more authentically than Cassidy Scheer. The son of a four-time log-rolling champion, Cassidy held his first ax at age four, going on to star in family lumberjack shows, excel in log rolling, and win ten world titles in tree climbing. Switching to sawing and chopping, the Minnesotan won the Stihl Timbersports US Championships and took silver in the Lumberjack World Championships just four years after qualifying for the US league.

"I love competing in these sports and enjoy the lifestyle that goes with it, which is about being healthy and active," he says.

"Many people have climbed a tree, chopped firewood, or maybe thrown an ax and, like rodeo, lumberjack sports draw on traditional jobs with an interesting history, which are aesthetically pleasing, too. I've lived in a city, so I understand the human need to reconnect with nature, and being a lumberjack offers so much pleasure: It's a great way of life."

Want to make like a lumberjack or Jill yourself? Here are Cassidy's top tips for living the lumberjack dream:

GET OUTDOORS

"Growing up in a small, rural town in Wisconsin, surrounded by forests, lakes, and rivers, I spent a lot of time outdoors hunting, fishing, and skiing. I don't hunt now but still love being

Lumberjacks relax in the bunkhouse at the Military Spruce Logging Camp in Hoquiam, Washington, during World War I, 1917.

From learning the basics of holding an ax to competing in timbersports, Cassidy Scheer has embraced the lumberjack lifestyle since he was a child.

outside in nature, connecting with things that are more tangible and visceral. I spend a lot of time foraging for wild mushrooms. My favorite days are in spring and fall, hiking through the state's magnificent white pine trees. I'll go out with a daypack and a cast-iron pan, catch a fish, forage some mushrooms, and cook them up out in the woods. It's an amazing, immersive outdoor experience, and I love it."

TRAIN SMART

"I'm constantly thinking about achieving the right balance in my training schedule, ensuring I do enough exercise to be as athletic as possible, but also refining my technique and how I present the ax and saw to the wood. The more you train in both areas, the better you'll be.

"Good mechanics on an ax swing or saw stroke will achieve more when you're cutting wood than just brute force, but once you've honed your technique, strength and power will help. I work on the movements used for chopping and sawing, such as explosive rotational power, which comes from the hips and core, and strengthening my legs. Cross-country skiing helps for endurance and hockey improves agility and hand-eye coordination. I do sprint training, weights, and plyometric

exercises to increase power and physicality, to be as fast, strong, and agile as possible."

STYLE IT OUT

"I really like an outdoor, refined style and traditional, rustic clothing brands like L.L.Bean, Best Made, Orvis, and Filson. I've been into raw, denim jeans for a while and particularly love the flannel double-down look, layering different colored and patterned flannels over each other. It's like matching two hardwoods on a piece of furniture. Wood always goes well with wood, no matter the color or pattern. I went through a 'metrosexual' phase at college, so I love the 'lumbersexual' trend. I'm one of the louder, more flamboyant guys in the community. I do celebration dances and compete in red plaid tights, which has become my signature look, and also rock a mullet. If you feel good, you'll perform well, so my competition clothes need to be comfortable and allow for maximum mobility, too."

EAT A BALANCED DIET

"I'm less meticulous about nutrition than other areas of my training because I'm a massive foodie and love rich, decadent,

ABOVE: Pictured here is a sunset view from Cassidy's cabin in Wisconsin. RIGHT: Cassidy designed his Scandi-inspired lakefront cabin himself.

and exotic meals! This usually takes precedent over eating the right amount of carbs and protein, although in the run-up to a competition, I pay more attention to the macronutrients consumed. I cut out junk food and eat cleaner, adding more fruit and vegetables, but still enjoy a glass of wine, a craft beer, or brandy—it's all about balance. Wisconsin is the 'Dairy State,' so I drink a lot of milk and eat around 4,000 calories a day, which I need to maintain my weight of 210 pounds (95 kg). It was easier to party and recover quickly in my twenties, but I'm more results-oriented now, so I don't drink much before a competition—but we definitely celebrate when it's over!"

LIVE THE LIFE YOU LOVE

"My apartment is in the suburbs of Minneapolis, and I'm one of the few 'urban lumberjacks'. Here I can access nearby training areas and timber, and I'm near to another competitor, so we train together. But I love spending time at my lakefront cabin in Hayward, which I designed myself, taking inspiration from Scandinavian summer cottages. My main career is real estate, and I'm designing more cabins which will be for sale, but this is somewhere I escape to. Nothing beats a cabin in the woods as the perfect lumberjack hideaway."

LUMBER CAMP CUISINE

With long days focused on logging, food was an important part of every lumberjack's life, providing fuel for forestry and a much-needed distraction from the backbreaking work

Laboring in the woods as a lumberjack for 10 or 12 hours a day was hungry work, with snow and rain adding to the demands on the body. The men needed plenty of food, or "chuck," to power them through, and mealtimes were the highlight of the day, offering a break from the routine of chopping and sawing.

In the early years of forestry in Maine, where commercial logging in the United States began, conditions for the lumberjacks were brutal, with the remoteness of the camps hindering the supply of good, fresh food. Pork, beans, and bread were the staple, cooked by a hired boy or sometimes by the men themselves. Other nonperishables in camp included baked codfish, pickled beef, flapjacks, sourdough biscuits, molasses, and tea.

By 1870, "all the common and substantial articles of food and drink" were on offer in the camps of the Great Lakes states, while in Canada a "revolution in camp diet" took place around 1880. The food in the New England camps improved in the early 1900s after legislation was brought in. It's estimated most loggers consumed at least 5,000 to 6,000 calories a day, eating an early breakfast at camp, a morning snack and dinner (what we call lunch) out in the woods, and a hearty evening supper (what we call dinner) at the camp when they returned.

BARRELS AND BELLIES

Feeding a large crew of loggers—with seventy-five to 100 men in camp—was a challenge. The cook and their assistant "cookees" worked hard, toiling over an open fire or a cast-iron range, to keep serving pots and platters replenished. Food was generally plain but wholesome, and the hungry lumberjacks devoured it all. Having a good cook in camp was a blessing, with poor chefs labeled as "belly robbers" by the men. Mealtimes at camp were quiet, aside from the clanking of cutlery on metal dishes, with talking at times forbidden in the dining room or mess hall in an attempt to discourage fights. Time limits were often set for finishing food, too; the busy kitchen staff wanting the men away so they could move on to other tasks.

Historic records reveal the foods that shanty boys ate in camp. Between 1875 and 1878, the annual consumption of the 1,200 workers at California's Sierra Flume and Lumber Company included 75 tons of beef, 75 of flour, 10 of beans, 20 of potatoes, 5 of butter, and 5 of dried fruit. In West Virginia in 1907, a smaller crew of forty-five men ate a tub of lard, a sack of turnips, a sack of onions, a box of yeast,

BUNYAN'S KITCHEN

The myth of Paul Bunyan helped to carve out the image of the constantly hungry lumberjack. Raised on a daily diet of 50 eggs and 10 containers of potatoes, the logger's kitchen covered 10 square miles, while his insatiable appetite for flapjacks was legendary.

The dining room at a lumber camp near Effie, Minnesota, 1937.

The camp cook summons the men for their evening meal with his Gabriel horn in the camp near Effie.

a case of cream, a barrel of sweet potatoes, seven sacks of Irish potatoes, a case of pears, a case of peaches, a case of tomatoes, two cases of eggs, a barrel of apples, 112 pounds (51 kg) of cabbage, a case of corn, 22 pounds (10 kg) of cakes, 10 pounds (5 kg) of tea, twelve cases of strawberries, two barrels of flour, 15 cans of baking powder, and 300 pounds (136 kg) of beef—in one week.

PINES AND PROVISIONS

An article titled "Among the Michigan Pines," written in 1885 by Boston-native

NOSH NICKNAMES

Lumberjacks had nicknames for food, including gravel (salt), sand (sugar), stove lids or sweat pads (pancakes), cackleberries (eggs), doorknobs (biscuits), goldfish (canned salmon), logging berries (stewed prunes), Murphys (potatoes), redlead (ketchup), slush or blackjack (coffee) and swamp water (tea).

Charles Ellis for local newspaper *The Chicago Current*, noted that the lumberjacks he'd visited at a Michigan camp were healthy and ate well: "The amount of work that a man or horse can do in the woods or elsewhere will depend entirely upon the amount of food that he can digest, over and above what is actually necessary to keep him in good condition in a state of inactivity. As regards these lumbermen, it is safe to say that they are physically strong and well, for only such can endure the work."

In his column, Charles noted that the fifty-five men wolfed down the following provisions during 20 weeks in camp:

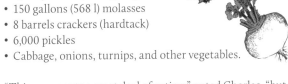

- 30 barrels flour
- 500 lb tea
- 22 barrels salt pork
- 4,000 pounds (1,814 kg) fresh meat
- 15 barrels beef
- 150 pounds (68 kg) baking powder
- 1,200 pounds (544 kg) lard
- 400 pounds (181 kg) butter
- 300 bushels potatoes
- 30 bushels beans
- 1,200 pounds (544 kg) sugar
- 150 gallons (568 l) molasses
- 8 barrels crackers (hardtack)
- 6,000 pickles
- Cabbage, onions, turnips, and other vegetables.

"This represents a great deal of eating," noted Charles, "but the work done will balance it off."

WHAT'S COOKIN'?
Here is a typical day's sustenance in the lumber camp:

BREAKFAST
For breakfast, taken around 6:00 a.m., the camp cook would rustle up oatmeal or cornmeal with sugar or molasses, flapjacks (or pancakes), sausages, ham or salt pork, baked beans, biscuits, potatoes, doughnuts, and prunes, all served with strong coffee.

DINNER (LUNCH)
The loggers stopped for a morning snack of bread and molasses with tea and carried on working until dinner arrived at midday, sometimes served around a fire. Cookees delivered the meals in pails, riding a horse and wagon or a sled, known as a "swingdingle." This hearty meal was often a beef vegetable stew with potatoes, onions, carrots, turnips, and cabbage, followed by pie and cookies. Ham and bean soup was also popular, served with more baked beans and sourdough bread.

SUPPER (DINNER)
When the Gabriel horn sounded to call the lumberjacks to dinner, the men would line up at the door of the cook shanty for a supper of meat (often roast or corned beef), potatoes, vegetables, bread or rolls, and desserts (usually pie or cake), along with tea or coffee. Then it was off to the campfire or men's camp to tell yarns, darn clothes, sing, or play music.

A man eats a well-earned supper in Effie, 1937.

PAUL BUNYAN'S
FAMOUS FLAPJACKS

Make a breakfast fit for a legendary lumberjack with this hearty recipe

According to lumberjack lore, Paul Bunyan's stove was the size of an acre, taller than a pine tree, and it took a whopping fifty men to grease the griddle. What's more, the legendary logger could wolf down fifty of his favorite flapjacks in one sitting. Elasticated pants at the ready? Let breakfast commence.

INGREDIENTS
Makes 12 small flapjacks
- 2 large eggs
- 1 cup (120 g) all-purpose flour
- ½ cup (80 g) cornmeal
- 2 teaspoons baking powder
- 1 teaspoon baking soda
- ¼ teaspoon salt
- 3 tablespoons sugar
- 1¼ cups (367 g) plain yogurt
- 6 tablespoons butter, melted

HOW TO DO IT
1. Preheat the oven to 200°F (93°C). Whisk together the flour, cornmeal, sugar, baking powder, baking soda, and salt in a large bowl.

2. In another bowl, mix together the yogurt and eggs with a fork, then stir this into the flour mixture and add the melted butter.

3. Heat a large greased, or nonstick skillet until hot.

4. For each flapjack, pour ¼ cup (60 ml) of batter into the skillet. Cook for three minutes until golden, then flip and cook on the other side.

5. Keep your flapjacks warm by placing them on a baking sheet or cooling rack in the oven while you cook the rest.

6. Serve with warm syrup, or add fruit and other toppings of your choice.

LAUREL FORK SAPSUCKERS
APPLE BUTTER

You can almost taste the fall leaves in this rich apple butter, made from an old family recipe at the Laurel Fork Sapsuckers Sugar Camp, high in the Appalachian Mountains of western Virginia

Surrounded by native red spruce forest, the Laurel Fork Sapsuckers Sugar Camp is known for its delicious pure Virginia maple syrup, made using traditional tree-tapping methods and wood-fired flat pans. The sustainable tree farm also produces a mean apple butter, perfect for spreading on toast or smothering over pancakes. Here's how to make it.

INGREDIENTS

Makes around 6 cups (1.4 l)
- 15 cooking apples
- 3 tablespoons granulated sugar
- 3 tablespoons brown sugar
- 2 teaspoons cinnamon
- A pinch of ground cloves
- Splash of bourbon or lemon juice

HOW TO DO IT

1. Peel and slice the apples, then chop the slices into smaller pieces, known as "snits."

2. Add the snits to a pan with a splash of water and cook until the juices have come out, stirring continuously so the mixture doesn't burn.

3. Add the sugar and spices, and simmer on a low heat until the apple butter is thick enough to hold its shape on a spoon and deep caramel in color. This should take around an hour.

4. Add a splash of bourbon or lemon juice to zing up your sauce.

5. Pour the apple butter into glass airtight jars and keep in the fridge for up to two weeks.

6. Spread the apple butter on toast, stir a dollop into your cereal, eat it with cheese, or use it as a topping for pancakes or waffles.

SUPERSIZED
The Laurel Fork Sapsuckers Sugar Camp team makes 240 pints (113 l) of apple butter each year, using 20 bushels of apples, a 45-gallon (170 l) copper kettle, and a wooden stirrer over 7 feet (2 m) long.

SPRUCE UP YOUR LIFE

If you ever find yourself lost in the woods, never fear. A simple spruce brew will not only help you stay warm, it will give your immune system a boost, too

Ever wondered how you'd survive alone, without food or a phone in the forest? Spruces and pines have long been used by indigenous peoples as a food source, for making drinks, and for healing (trees with ancient bark-peeling scars are still common in old-growth pine forests), so these prickly powerhouses could save the day if you find yourself in a tight spot. Many parts of the trees are edible, from the inner bark—which is packed with stored carboyhdrates, dietary fiber, and minerals—to the pollen and pine cone seeds, and the needles are a great source of vitamin C.

POWERFUL POTIONS

Canada's First Nations people were making spruce drinks for generations before French explorer, Jacques Cartier, arrived on his second voyage to the New World in 1535. When scurvy broke out, killing twenty-five of the 110-strong crew, Domagaya, the son of Iroquois chief Donnacona, showed the sailors how to make a vitamin C–packed potion from local pines. Believed to be spruce beer, the brew saved the lives of the remaining men. Cartier repaid them in true colonial style, kidnapping Donnacona and nine of his tribe, including his sons, and sending them back to France, where all but one died.

VITAMIN TEA

Steep a spoonful of chopped pine or spruce needles in a cup of hot water for 10 minutes to make a tea that's packed with vitamin C. Just one cup contains as much as five times your daily requirement.

In addition to serving as a food source, spruce trees are used to produce paper and lumber.

BIG-TIME BREWERS

- British explorer Captain James Cook made spruce beer in New Zealand during his second voyage in 1773, boiling spruce branches and tea plants with yeast and molasses.
- The first President of the United States, General George Washington, served spruce beer to his troops in 1775 at the start of the American War of Independence.
- United States founding father Benjamin Franklin made up a brew from essence of spruce and lots of molasses, which inspired modern craft beers.

HOP TO IT

In her 1796 book, *American Cookery*, which features Native American recipes, Amelia Simmons describes how to brew a spruce beer:

- "Take four ounces of hops, let them boil half an hour in one gallon of water, strain the hop water, then add 16 gallons of warm water, two gallons of molasses, eight ounces of essence of spruce, dissolved in one quart of water.
- Put it in a clean cask, then shake it well together, add half a pint of emptins [yeast or leavening], then let it stand and work one week. If it's very warm weather, less time will do. When it is drawn off to bottle, add one spoonful of molasses to every bottle."

VIKING VA-VA-VOOM

Ancient Scandinavians brewed beer from the young shoots of Norway spruce trees, convinced it increased their fertility and strength in battle.

NATURAL REMEDY

Spruce needles have traditionally been used as an antiseptic, expectorant, antibiotic, and sedative.

CANOE GLUE

Indigenous people used the sap from the spruce trees as glue for their birch bark canoes, while lumberjacks would chew on it like gum to freshen their breath.

BESTO FOR PESTO

The young spruce tips that grow through in spring can be used raw in salads or pesto, or cooked to make syrups and jams and flavor dishes—they're especially good in Thai cuisine.

WARNING: PICK YOUR PINE

Before you go a-foraging in the woods, make sure you know your pines. Not all species are safe to eat—including the Norfolk Island pine, the yew, and ponderosa pine—so correct identification from a reputable tree book or guide is crucial. Always consult a medical professional before using any kind of plant for healing, and pregnant women should avoid eating or drinking pine or spruce needles.

HOW TO

EAT LIKE A CHAMP

Want to build some lumberjack-sized strength and agility? It's not all about stacking steak and eggs for breakfast. Fitness expert, author, and founder of Fit Men Cook, Kevin Curry, shares his healthy tips for eating like a champion

Philadelphia-born fitness expert Kevin Curry overcame severe depression and weight issues by turning to healthy eating and a diet packed with tasty nutritious foods. Along with a popular Instagram account and YouTube channels, Kevin has a FitMenCook app, which has reached number one in the health category in over eighty countries, and a best-selling book, *Fit Men Cook*. This guy knows his proteins, his micronutrients, and all the good stuff lumberjacks should be loading in between.

STRIKE A BALANCE

"Whether you're training at an Olympic level or just starting to think about your nutrition more seriously, it's essential to understand the different kinds of calories out there. Wielding saws and axes means you're going to require a high-carb diet to fuel you throughout the day, with a healthy complement of protein to help build and recover muscle tissue. But lumberjacks aren't bodybuilders (even though some may look the part), so you want to have a balanced amount of fat in your diet, too."

BUILD MUSCLE, STAY AGILE

"Swinging an ax consistently for an hour will burn around 350 to 500 calories, and the average male lumberjack eats around 4,000 calories a day to get in competition shape, while competing females will eat around 2,500 to 3,000 calories a day. For both, I'd recommend starting with 2.5 grams of protein per kilogram of body weight, 4–7 grams of carbs, and

OPPOSITE: Men at a logging camp near Effie, Minnesota, dish out and serve food, 1937. **ABOVE:** Kevin designs recipes that help to build healthy bodies. **RIGHT:** Plant-based meals pack a protein punch that's just as effective as red meat, poultry, or fish.

0.5–2 grams of fat for that kind of work. That's similar to how bodybuilders eat to put on massive muscle, while staying lean enough to be agile."

RETHINK THE "LUMBERJACK BREAKFAST"

"Let's reconsider the lumberjack's breakfast. Here in America, some diners have created 'lumberjack-themed' breakfasts that are high in carbs and fat and low in protein. Essentially, the protein and fat distribution needs to flip. Instead, try something like my High-Protein Egg, Yam, and Cheese Jar. Not only is it effortless to make (and eat on the go!), but it also has a much healthier split, with 41 grams of protein, 45 grams of carbs, and 15 grams of fat." *See the recipe on page 109.*

CHALLENGE STEREOTYPES

"Lumberjacks have an image in our culture: they're big, burly, bearded, and they eat a dozen eggs and a pack of bacon for breakfast. But stereotypes often don't do anyone any favors. Alternative sources of protein can work just as effectively as red meat, poultry, or fish. Not only are plant-based protein sources like peas, edamame, and beans more sustainable, but you can also use them to make delicious meals that pack a protein punch, while helping you maintain a balanced diet. I enjoy bodybuilding and high-intensity interval training, and my muscles definitely didn't shrink on my four-day High-Protein Vegan Meal Plan, so I promise yours won't either!"

This Salisbury mushrooms and peas is a dish that follows the guidelines of the Mediterranean diet.

EMBRACE THE MEDITERRANEAN

"I started by focusing on macronutrients, because that's where we begin when we're discussing dieting or setting nutrition goals for specific purposes. But micronutrients are just as essential, which is why it's time to say goodbye to a 'meat 'n' potatoes' lifestyle. Here's why I love the Mediterranean diet so much, and why it's still the reigning diet year after year. Not only is it easy to maintain as a lifestyle, but it's also full of bright, vibrant, and flavorful foods, like cucumbers, tomatoes, and red onions, that help to ensure your body's getting all the vitamins and minerals it needs. Plus, it never gets boring. And if there's one thing I can't stand, it's eating boring food!"

HIIT THE TOP

"Now let's get outside of the kitchen for a minute and think about using our bodies to stay healthy, build muscle, and get into great competitive shape. High-intensity interval training (HIIT) workouts are fantastic ways to build muscle, because the movements involved usually activate a wide variety of muscles all at once—not unlike competitive lumberjack sports, or the daily demands of the logging profession itself. You won't gain the same kind of muscle mass you'd build benching your one-rep max, but you will tap into highly effective, even explosive power."

ADD A KICK TO YOUR H20

"Lastly—and this is probably the most important tip—remember to stay hydrated. Drinking enough water throughout the day prevents injury by protecting your joints, keeping them lubricated and dispersing nutrients throughout your body. Hydration is so overlooked, but so important that I even include a water-tracking feature in my app. If you're struggling to stay committed to drinking water throughout the day, try adding some mint leaves, which will give it a refreshing kick (and freshen your breath, too), or even more creative ingredients like jalapeños: spicy, but as a lumberjack or Jill, you can take it!"

Stay hydrated and give your water a kick with mint, cucumber, or jalapeño.

THE HEALTHY LUMBERJACK BREAKFAST
HIGH-PROTEIN EGG, YAM, AND CHEESE JAR

INGREDIENTS
Makes 1 serving
- 2 eggs
- 3 egg whites
- 4 ounces (100 g) yam
  (or sweet potato)
- ¼ cup diced red bell pepper
- 2 tablespoons diced red onion
- ⅓ cup shredded spinach
- ¼ cup reduced-fat
  shredded parmesan
  cheese (optional)
- 1½ teaspoons herb seasoning
- Pinch of sea salt

HOW TO DO IT
1. Peel then grate the yam into a bowl
and set it aside.

2. In a separate bowl, beat the eggs
and egg whites with the salt and
herb seasoning.

3. Add the bell pepper, red onion,
spinach, and a little parmesan (if
desired) to the eggs, and mix together.

4. Spray an ovenproof jar (at least 12
ounces [355 ml] in size) with olive oil,
then add the grated yam. Pat it down so
it covers the bottom of the jar.

5. Pour the egg and veggie mixture
into the jar, then garnish with a
sprinkle of parmesan.

6. Place the jar on a baking sheet and
bake in the oven for around 30 minutes
at 375°F (190°C).

HEALTHY FORESTS, HEALTHY PLANET

The nineteenth-century logging boom changed landscapes across North America, and deforestation remains an issue of global concern today. Can sustainable forestry balance the economic benefits of timber with the environmental value of trees?

Since the first English settlers arrived in Jamestown, Virginia, in 1607, it's estimated that America has lost somewhere between 75 and 90 percent of its virgin forest. Indigenous peoples farmed holistically and were hunter-gatherers, working in harmony with the land, but the new arrivals voraciously tore through the New World, converting ancient forests to farmlands, and logging like there was no tomorrow. In some regions, all that remained were vast areas of "cutover," a barren landscape of stumps, stripped of all life.

Legal forest and land protections, introduced in the mid-1800s and subsequent years, arrested what could have been total annihilation. The world's first national park, Yellowstone, was established in 1872, and the preservation of its two million acres is the reason the UNESCO World Heritage Site remains one of the few intact ecosystems on Earth today. Elsewhere, a fragile balance remains in play.

ANCIENT FORESTS

United Nations data shows there are more forested lands in North America today than 100 years ago, and between 2010 and 2020 forest cover in the United States increased 0.03 percent annually. Meanwhile, according to the Canadian Forest Service, the area harvested in 2018 represented 0.2 percent of the total area of forest land, with the harvested area promptly replanted.

Leaving carbon "locked" in the forest is a good idea. The Pacific Northwest is home to some of the highest carbon density forests in the world, where trees can store carbon for more than 800 years. Stretching from northern California to Alaska, this is where you'll find some of America's last remaining old-growth forests, which are still actively targeted for logging.

A 2018 report by researchers at Oregon State University and the University of Idaho found that logging is by far the number one source of greenhouse gas emissions in Oregon, emitting 33 million tons of CO_2 a year, almost as much as one of the world's dirtiest coal plants, the Taichung Power Plant in Taiwan.

In 2019, the Center for Sustainable Economy concluded that the logging industry emitted enormous quantities of greenhouse gas.

FORESTS TO FARMLAND

While unsustainable and illegal logging are having a devastating effect on the world's forests, the biggest global driver of deforestation is agriculture: converting forests to farmland and grazing land for livestock.

OPPOSITE TOP: A forest in British Columbia, where harvested areas are quickly replanted.
OPPOSITE BOTTOM: A truck hauls salvaged logs from Montana's Lolo National Forest. Salvage logging recovers trees damaged by storms or fires.

Focusing on the industry in North Carolina, the study found that 201,000 acres of forest are cleared each year, producing 44 million tons of carbon dioxide. The United National Food and Agriculture Organization (FAO), meanwhile, estimates that the world has lost around 420 million hectares of forest since 1990, mainly in Africa and South America. And while trees are being replanted, industrial forest lands store much less carbon than the native forests they've replaced, and sustain less biodiversity—one million species are known to be at risk of extinction.

The good news is that now the data is out there, the damage can begin to be repaired. The ancient forests that have been lost will never return, but with hindsight and new science on our side, we can plant the seeds of a greener tomorrow.

MAN OF THE WILDERNESS

Known as the "Father of the National Parks," Scottish-American author, botanist, and early conservationist John Muir helped to secure protection for America's wilderness areas, including Sequoia, General Grant, and Yosemite National Parks and Yosemite's Mariposa Grove, a magical forest of 500 Giant Sequoias, home to the 3,000-year-old "Grizzly Giant."

In his essay, *God's First Temples; How Shall We Preserve Our Forests?*, published in 1876, John warned of the dangers of destroying forests, "the most destructible of the natural resources." In a brilliant early analysis of trees' contribution to the Earth's "climate, soil, and streams," he warned: "Our forest belts are being burned and cut down and wasted like a field of unprotected grain, and once destroyed, can never be wholly restored."

Going on to found the Sierra Club in 1892, to "do something for wildness and make the mountains glad," John helped to preserve precious habitat and inspire awe and admiration for land that the country's Native people had been protecting as responsible stewards for thousands of years.

TOP: Conservationist John Muir protected America's wilderness.
ABOVE: Freshly cut forest near Effie, Minnesota, 1937.

SO WHAT IS SUSTAINABLE FORESTRY?

According to North America's Sustainable Forestry Initiative (SFI), which works with the forest sector, conservationists, governments and communities to advance the sustainable use of forest lands, sustainable forestry ensures the long-term health of forests while providing social, economic, and environmental benefits from timber harvesting. Management decisions and activities are based on scientific research, rigorous planning processes, certification standards, and meaningful public consultation. They also support ecosystem services, like water purification and carbon storage, while maintaining the health and diversity of forests. Replanting after harvesting trees helps forests, and the habitats they contain, to regenerate. This is one of the core principles of sustainable forest management.

Loggers are key players in helping to solve some of today's biggest sustainability challenges.

WHY DO WE NEED FORESTS?

Forests are one of the planet's most important natural resources. They're the ultimate "renewable" and one of the greatest tools in fighting climate change. They clean the air we breathe, filter the water we drink, and support educational opportunities for today's youth.

HOW DO TREES FIGHT CLIMATE CHANGE?

Protecting the world's trees is one of the most cost-effective forms of climate action. Forests act as carbon sinks, absorbing roughly two billion tons of carbon dioxide each year. They're also increasingly managed for resilience in the face of climate change's effects. Practicing climate-smart forestry focuses on actions like increasing the diversity of tree species to make them more resilient to wildfires and pests. According to the US Forest Service, 100 trees remove 53 tons (48 metric tons) of carbon dioxide and 430 pounds (195 kg) of other air pollutants every year. If we want to tackle the issues of climate change, water quality, waste reduction, and species loss, taking good care of the world's forests is fundamental.

HOW DOES THIS "GREEN" APPROACH HELP COMMUNITIES AND WILDLIFE?

Sustainable forestry is focused on encouraging a positive relationship between people and forests, balancing their needs, and aiming to create both a sustainable marketplace and healthy landscapes. Purchasing products from a sustainably managed and certified source helps to conserve the planet's precious wildlife and natural resources.

Communities rely on forests for their livelihoods and economic development, sustainable products, recreational benefits, and human health. These links have always been important, but are even more relevant in today's increasingly connected and developing world.

HOW DO LOGGERS PRACTICE SUSTAINABLE FORESTRY TODAY?

Logging companies need to ensure they're implementing forestry practices that protect the environment every day. Sustainable management enhances water quality, protects wildlife habitat, accounts for wildfire risk, counters invasive species, and recognizes indigenous rights, accounting for the social and economic well-being of workers and local communities.

Forest certification standards, such as the international Forest Stewardship Council (FSC) and the SFI, are there to help ensure forests are managed sustainably. The SFI trains thousands of loggers in sustainable forest practices each year. When they're aware of the importance of their role and responsibilities, they're better equipped to protect the environment.

OLD TREES: NEW LIFE

Every tree has a tale to tell, and by salvaging and repurposing vintage lumber, Robert Rising—"The Black Lumberjack"—is keeping their stories alive

Think of the things our world's ancient trees have seen: the animals and people that have come and gone, the ebb and flow of seasons, conflicts, celebrations, and generations working the land. Standing tall, they provide shelter and shade, stabilize soil, and allow us to breathe. Cut for timber, they fulfill other roles, providing homes and protection, buoying ships, and shoring up sacred spires. And crafted into furniture or art, they bring comfort, pleasure, and delight. But when their usefulness is served, they're too often destroyed: burned, pulped, wood chipped, or turned into mulch.

Robert Rising is on a mission to change their destinies. NYCitySlab, his mill yard in Dover Plains, New York, is where dejected, discarded, and abandoned trees are reborn and sent back out into the world to create stories anew. Here, the urban lumberjack tells his own tale.

CHALLENGING TRADITION

"I've always loved being in the forest. Trees are good for the soul and when I'm among them I'm at peace, but it was while I was working at the bar in New York's Four Seasons Hotel that I had my 'lightbulb' moment about working with wood.

"I'd decided to build my dream house up state and wanted to fill it with cool stuff, like cherry wood cabinets and coun- tertops and walnut tables—but I couldn't find them anywhere. On my drives out of the city, I started to notice trucks on the side of the road, wood chipping logs for mulch. I couldn't believe these beautiful trees were going to end up shredded in the dirt, so I spoke to some of the workers and asked if they'd let me have some of the logs for the house. They agreed, so I found a local man who'd be able to saw them for me, but soon realized that by the time I'd paid him to do it, I could buy the equipment and do it myself. I bought a saw and got to work, making my own slabs and furniture from reclaimed wood. I taught myself about the different tree species, picking up tips on YouTube and Google. The more I did it, the better I became at it.

"News spread about what I was doing, and someone bought two cherry slabs from me to use in their house. That's when I realized I could turn my love of reclaimed wood into a business. Instead of building the house, I moved locally, opened up a lumber yard, and NYCitySlab was born. I also earned myself a new title after people saw me towing big logs on my trailer. They'd shout, 'Yo! Black Lumberjack!' as I drove by. The name came straight from the streets of Mt. Vernon, New York, and stuck. There aren't many of us around, so I'm happy to be changing the traditional image and challenging stereotypes."

Robert creates bespoke pieces from reclaimed wood at his NYCitySlab mill yard in New York.

The NYCitySlab lumberyard is stocked with timber from over twenty-five native tree species.

REIMAGINING THE PAST FOR THE PRESENT

"Fourteen years on, NYCitySlab employs five people, has a full metal shop, a showroom in Yonkers, and a yard stocked with timber from over twenty-five species of New York City and northeast native trees. All the wood we use is local and reclaimed. We rescue fallen or diseased trees from parks and yards that would otherwise be used for firewood and give them a new lease of life. Homeowners also contact us to salvage trees that have been in their gardens for years and have sentimental value, but for some reason need to be removed. We transform them into something special that goes back into their home and can last a lifetime.

"If a tree or a beam could tell the story of the life it's lived, it would be pretty amazing. I always think about the things the tree has gone through, or the things a building has seen, when I'm working. It's very satisfying to save all these amazing trees from being chipped and preserve some of their history—I'm just sorry I can't save them all.

"We collect timber from old buildings around the city, too, and document where our lumber is from, so our customers know the story of each piece. We mainly work with hardwoods. Our native dark woods—walnut and cherry—are both wonderful, and I love the spalting [coloration caused by fungi] that you find in some of the sugar trees, like maple, beech, and elm. But what's important is the individuality of each tree.

"On site, we have a sawmill, lathes, planer, jointers, a kiln, sanders, a milling machine, anvil, and forge. We work with customers to choose the wood, then design unique pieces for their home, office, or public spaces, from kitchen surfaces to bar tops, and coffee counters to conference tables. We've created 86 benches made from thermally modified ash trees as part of the regeneration of Roberto Clemente Plaza in the

Robert and his team create customized furniture for homes and businesses.

Bronx, and contributed pieces to both the Whitney Museum of American Art and The Museum of Modern Art in NYC. We also have a DIY program, where we open up our workshop to people who want to come in and personally make their own items, with a bit of guidance from us."

INSPIRING A NEW GENERATION

"It's important for me to teach young people of color the essential woodworking skills needed to succeed in the industry, so we're setting up inspiring educational and training programs with local high schools and colleges.

"Working with your hands, making your own goods, and upcycling have become popular, which makes sense for the environment, and for the future of the planet. It's also incredibly rewarding. But traditionally, people of color haven't been lumberjacks, or woodworkers, because historically—as in so

many areas of life—systemic racism prevented those opportunities from being available to us. African slaves helped to build some of the nation's most incredible monuments, including The White House and the United States Capitol in Washington, DC, and George Washington's own home Mount Vernon, in Virginia, but African-Americans have been largely boxed out of profiting from working in carpentry or construction.

"We need to rectify that, which is why I'm trying my best to initiate change. There are so many people of color who are passionate, talented, and who can excel in this industry if they're given the chance. The difference between those who make it and those who don't is that they have the will to try and to learn. When I dived into this, it was about necessity and a dream. So if you believe in something, educate yourself about it, and then fight for it until your dream becomes a reality. It might not happen quickly, but it will happen."

THE JUMPING FRENCHMEN OF MAINE

When a mysterious affliction spread through a remote logging community in New England in the late 1800s, Dr. George Millard Beard ventured into the woods to investigate ...

"They could not help striking their best friend, if near them, when ordered ... It was dangerous to startle them in any way when they had an ax or knife in their hands ..."

While it could easily be the screen direction in a script for the latest lost-in-the-woods-teen-slasher, this alarming description is actually from an American neurologist, based on his own observations of a strange phenomenon he experienced in an isolated lumberjack camp in Maine.

Rumors were emerging from the forests of New England, about a community of French-Canadian loggers suffering from an unexplained syndrome, which caused them to exhibit an extreme reaction when startled. At the annual Meeting of the American Neurological Association in 1878, Dr. George M. Beard announced his intention to visit the logging camp in Moosehead Lake to observe and examine the afflicted.

George M. Beard.

LIFE ON A KNIFE EDGE

Known as "The Jumping Frenchmen of Maine," the lumberjacks demonstrating the syndrome displayed an exaggerated response to loud noises, sudden commands, or unexpected contact. The reactions ranged from screaming, to flailing their limbs, hitting things or people, throwing objects, and, of course, jumping. They would also often repeat an order they'd been given like a parrot (a condition called echolalia), while making violent, muscular movements. Reporting on his findings at the camp, Dr. Beard observed: "Whatever order was given to them was at once obeyed. Thus one of the Jumpers who ... was told to throw [a knife] ... threw it quickly so that it stuck in the house opposite [and] at the same time, he repeated the order to throw it with a cry of alarm ... He also threw away his pipe, which he was filling ... when he was clapped upon the shoulder."

JUMPING TO A CONCLUSION

Of the fifty people Dr. Beard observed, he found fourteen cases of the syndrome in people from four families, suggesting a possible genetic link, although this wasn't proven. Certain medical conditions can cause excessive startling, such as magnesium deficiency, tetanus, or degenerative brain disorders, but Dr. Beard speculated that the syndrome had developed due to the impact of living in remote isolation in camp. He also suggested it started in childhood, lasted a lifetime, and was more prevalent in men. The condition itself didn't harm the Jumpers, but such extreme reactions could sometimes put them—and those around them—in danger.

"Two Jumpers standing near each other were told to strike, and they struck each other very forcibly," Dr. Beard recorded. "When the commands are uttered in a quick, loud voice, the Jumper repeats the order . . . They could not help repeating the word of sound that came from the person that ordered them, any more than they could help striking, dropping, throwing, jumping, or starting." The men didn't just respond to commands or human voices. Any loud or sudden noise could spark a reaction. As Dr. Beard noted: "It was not necessary that the sound should come from a human being . . . One of these Jumpers came very near to cutting his throat while shaving on hearing a door slam. They have been known to strike their fists against a red-hot stove, to jump into fire and into water."

EXTREME SURPRISE

While humans have an inherent "startle response," there are several conditions that manifest a more extreme reaction to outside stimuli: hyperekplexia, a rare neurological disorder that causes patients to go rigid when surprised, sometimes falling face first onto the floor; startle epilepsy, when those affected experience seizures triggered by a sensory change such as taste, sound, pressure, or temperature; and the rare "jumping" reaction, experienced by the lumberjacks in Maine and a few other communities across the globe.

The condition was reported in other remote lumber camps in New England and Québec at that time, while similar variations include "latah" in Malaysia, "miryachit" in Siberia, and Louisiana's "Ragin' Cajuns."

CULTURAL CONDITIONING

Studying Dr. Beard's findings, French neurologist Gilles de la Tourette came to believe that the syndrome was part of the same group of illnesses as Tourette's, which affects the nervous system and is characterized by compulsive motor and vocal tics. While some of the jumping behaviors are similar to those exhibited by people with Tourette's, extreme stress, emotional tension, fatigue, and even cultural conditioning could also be factors to consider.

As recently as 2011, nineteen students and one adult at a school in Le Roy, New York, started exhibiting mysterious involuntary twitches, tics, and spasms. While just one student was diagnosed with Tourette's Syndrome, the others who had been displaying similar behaviors were diagnosed with conversion disorder.

Doctors concluded that psychological stress had caused the patients to suffer physical symptoms and mass psychogenic illness: the group, it was suggested, had been subconsciously copying each other. A rest from stress and social media was prescribed, along with treatment at a neurology clinic, and life returned to normal.

While building an Instagram following may not have been a concern for the Jumping Frenchmen of Maine, the hardships that they experienced working in one of North America's most remote regions may have been enough to trigger the strange syndrome, which scientists are still striving to understand today.

JUMPERS UNDER FIRE

Robert E. Pike, who wrote about life in the lumber camps of New England in his 1967 book *Tall Trees, Tough Men*, told how the Jumping Frenchmen of Maine often found

STEAM POWER

Moosehead Lake is the largest lake in Maine. In the early 19th century, it was the only way to reach many of the state's remote logging camps, with early steamboats hauling supplies and passengers to the camps, and towing booms of logs to the sawmills.

themselves the victims of practical jokes at the hands of the other lumberjacks.

"If a Jumper was shaving, or whistling, or just sitting on a riverbank, and someone came up behind him suddenly and cried: 'Jump into the river!' (or 'into the fire,' if there was a fire), in he'd jump."

If the camp cook was a Jumper, "the men would wait until [the cook] was about to place a dish of soup or some other spilly food on the table and then say, 'Drop it!' and down it would come, right down the neck of the nearest man."

Sometimes a lumberjack would pretend to strike the man sitting next to him. "Every Jumper in the line would turn and strike at his neighbor. Or a man would pretend to throw his pipe on the floor. Then the Jumpers could not help dashing down their own pipes."

ABOVE: Using pikes, workers keep logs moving during a spring pulpwood drive held in Maine, 1943. Pulpwood refers to wood that is intended for paper production. **RIGHT:** A team of lumberjacks posing with a felled giant sequoia tree, 1905.

PILE HIGH CLUB

Gary Tallman may have the most artistic farm in Montana, thanks to the amazing mosaics he creates with the logs in his woodpile

Nestled amid the pines and aspen of the Little Belt Mountains in Montana, Gary Tallman's farm holds a lumber-size secret: an 8 x 13-foot (2 x 4 m) mosaic, constructed from wood gathered in the local forest. These ornate log piles have made Gary somewhat of a local celebrity, although the modest octogenarian fails to see what the fuss is about.

"I started building them just because I enjoyed doing it, and to send photographs of them to my grandkids," he says. "It surprises me that people are fascinated by them. I never expected it to go this far. It's kind of embarrassing sometimes."

Preferring to keep his unique creations personal, Gary has twice politely declined invitations from the local Paris Gibson Square Museum of Art to create exhibition works.

With changing themes and motifs each year, the mosaics take Gary around twenty hours to make—not including the hours spent gathering, chopping, and sorting the wood, or drawing his preliminary sketches. Featuring owls, bears,

mountains, and trees, Gary's art is inspired by the surrounding wilderness and wildlife, and uses different-colored wood species, including cedar, larch, poplar, and cottonwood, to create the designs.

"We've always admired our woodpile, and there are so many tones in the timber," says Gary's wife, Marilyn. "Gary sees beauty in all kinds of things." It's not just wood that he uses to work his magic. There are sculptures made from old motor parts and even a stove around the farm—permanent exhibits that exist beyond the ephemeral woodpile, which diminishes each year, as winter sets in. Some artists would be sad to see their hard work go up in flames, but not Gary. As the last logs from his *Starry Night* mosaic head to the wood burner he smiles. "It was just another season, and just another woodpile."

Gary uses wood from local tree species to create unique nature scenes each year.

HOW TO TRAIN TO WIN

Nobody climbs to the top of the lumberjack tree without shedding a little blood, a lot of sweat, and even a few tears. But you can minimize the pain by making sure you train smart.

Elgan Pugh, the UK's greatest axman, is living proof that to be the best at something, you don't need start doing it while you're in diapers. Unlike some of his contemporary athletes who inherited a lumber sports family legacy, the thirty-eight-year-old five-time winner of the British Stihl Timbersports Championships didn't swing an ax until he was twenty-seven, but he's been making up for lost time ever since.

"Growing up in Wales as a farmer's son, I used to love visiting the Royal Welsh Show every year with my parents," recalls Elgan, speaking from his home in Bala, Wales. "I would watch the woodchopping displays for hours each year, but it wasn't until my late twenties that an ax demo team at another local show invited me to give it a go."

As a trained carpenter and owner of a construction company, weighing in at a strong 198–209 pounds (90–95 kg), Elgan was already in pretty good shape for lumber sports. After taking up the opportunity to join the Clwyd Axemen team for some training sessions, he soon discovered he also had the passion and talent he needed to succeed. Just two months later, Elgan was back at 2009's Royal Welsh Show as a competitor, where he came second in the underhand chop event.

Entering his first national lumber sport event in 2012, Elgan narrowly missed out on third place, which drove him to train harder. With no nationals in 2013, he focused on the 2014 competition, where he took silver. "To come second so soon after I started competing was great, but I'd done a lot of preparation, so it wasn't really what I was after!" laughs Elgan. Upping his training game, he returned the following year to claim the championship title, which he has won every year the event has been held since.

"The thrill of competing is all I need to keep me motivated and working hard. During the off-season, I'll do more mountain biking, road cycling, and weight training. In the months leading up to a competition, I'll spend hours practicing each of the events," says Elgan, who holds the British records for the stock saw, hot saw, and Champion's Trophy competitions. "I love having the opportunity to go up against some fantastic athletes. We're all competitive, but very supportive, too. It's a great sport to be part of."

Staying at the top of the game takes commitment and discipline, and while it's competing that drives Elgan to train, setting fitness goals can help you to achieve your own personal records, too. On the next page, Elgan shares some of his top training tips to get you in good shape, and remember: "It's never too late to try something new, so go for it."

A lumberjack competes in a woodchopping competition at an agricultural show in South Australia, 1917.

WARM UP

This is essential before you do any training. I'll go for a short jog, bike ride, or do some skipping for five minutes to get my blood pumping. Then I'll do a variety of gentle arm swings and shoulder rolls to loosen up: 10–15 forward, then the same in reverse.

MUSCLE POWER

I have a squat rack at home for weightlifting, and I do lots of dead lifts and squats—both great for building power. Try to include some squats and lunges in your workout to build up your leg muscles, adding a kettlebell or medicine ball for an extra challenge. Planks are great for working out your core, and side planks really strengthen your side muscles, which will help when you're chopping and sawing.

Before you start any new exercise routine, consult a medical professional. Increase weights and repetitions slowly, and always stop exercising and consult your doctor if you feel any pain.

BALL SLAM

Start with the medicine ball on the floor. Squat down to pick it up and then quickly lift it up above your head, before slamming it down onto the ground in front of you, as hard as you can. Keep your back straight and your legs and elbows slightly bent. You're aiming to improve your strength, stamina, and speed, so repeat the movement as fast as possible. Start with a 5-kilogram (11 lb.) ball and do around ten repetitions, then slowly build up the ball weight and reps. I use a 6-kilogram (13 lb.) ball and do around fifty slams each session. This means that when I come to lift a 3–3.5-kilogram (7–8 lb.) ax in a competition, it feels a lot lighter.

SHOULDER STRETCH

This is an easy but effective exercise to really stretch out the muscles in your shoulders and arms. Use a weightlifting bar, or even a broom, and drape your arms over the pole, until you feel a good—but not painful—stretch. Slowly rotate the upper body from the hips as far as you can, then hold the position for 10 seconds. Now, slowly rotate back to the center and then round to the other side, holding for another 10. This exercise isn't about speed or reps, but achieving a controlled, deep stretch.

RECOVERY TIPS

Eating a healthy diet, packed with lots of vitamins and minerals will help keep you in tip-top shape. I also take a multivitamin and an omega-3 complex for joints to help keep them supple. Good hydration is essential, so drink lots of water.

KETTLE SWING

Like the ball slam, this exercise will improve your chopping technique while giving you a full-body workout, but the movements are slower and more controlled. Start with the kettlebell on the ground in front of you and grip it in the way you would an ax, with your dominant hand at the top of the handle, and the other hand below it. Next, swing the kettlebell up above your head, replicating the arc you'd make when swinging an ax, keeping your legs and elbows bent. Swing the bell back down to just between your legs, without letting it touch the ground, then take it straight back up again. I do between fifty to 100 repetitions and lift a 16-kilogram (35 lbs.) kettlebell, but start with a weight you're comfortable with, and build up slowly.

WIND DOWN

Always leave some time to stretch properly after each training session, making sure you pay attention to your arm and leg muscles—you'll really appreciate this the next day.

TOP RIGHT: Elgan competes in the underhand chop competition at the 2018 Stihl Timbersports World Championship.
BOTTOM RIGHT: Elgan holds the British records in the stock saw, hot saw and Champions Trophy competitions.

SHANTY BOY SONGS

From melancholy Irish ballads to bawdy drinking ditties, lumberjacks loved to sing songs after a hard day's graft amid the pines. Fiddles at the ready...

Drawing on work experiences, the dangers of the job, drinking, and, of course, matters of the heart, lumberjack songs are as varied as those who would write and sing them.

European immigrants brought their music and tales to North America's logging camps, where lyrics were reworked to reflect the shanty boys' way of life. The lumberjacks also added bluegrass, Civil War songs, and spirituals into the mix.

Songs were sung in the evening beside the stove or around the campfire, as men sharpened axes, darned clothes, talked, told stories, and played cards. Accompanied by instruments,

including the fiddle, banjo, guitar, mouth organ, and even a hand saw played with a bow, the songs traveled with the lumberjacks as they moved from camp to camp, evolving as they'd go.

Lumberjacks have continued to feature in music genres from country to rock and rap, inspiring Johnny Cash's "Lumberjack," Jackyl's "The Lumberjack" (which includes an actual chainsaw solo), and Serum featuring Inja's "Lumberjackin'"—with Monty Python's "The Lumberjack Song" becoming a camp classic of a wholly irreverent kind.

In 2020, historic work songs made it into the mainstream, when #tiktokshanty went viral around the globe, thanks to the video-sharing platform, TikTok, with a nineteenth-century whaler's song, "Wellerman"—recorded by Scottish shanty-singing mailman, Nathan Evans—topping the charts in early 2021. Think you could be the new #lumberjackshantysensation? Get TikTokking with these tunes.

ONCE MORE A-LUMBERING GO

Traditional lumbertale "Once More a-Lumbering Go" was first featured in John S. Springer's 1851 book *Forest Life and Forest Trees*, under the title "The Logger's Boast." Recordings include a version by lumberjack Carl Lathrop recorded by Alan Lomax in 1938, another by "The Adirondack Minstrel" Lawrence Older from the 1960s, and a recent take by Minnesotan singer and musician Brian Miller.

Come all you sons of freedom and listen to my theme
Come all you roving lumberjacks that run the Saginaw stream
We'll cross the Tittabawassee where the mighty waters flow
And we'll roam the wild woods over and once more
   a-lumbering go

[Chorus]
And once more a-lumbering go
And we'll range the wild woods over
And once more a-lumbering go

When the white frost hits the valley, and the snow conceals
   the woods
The lumberjack has enough to do to find his family food
No time he has for pleasure or to hunt the buck and doe
He will roam the wild woods over and once more
   a-lumbering go

[Repeat chorus]

With our crosscut saws and axes we will make the woods resound
And many a tall and stately tree will come crashing to
   the ground
With cant hooks on our shoulders to our boot tops deep in snow
We will roam the wild woods over and once more
   a-lumbering go

[Repeat chorus]

You may talk about your farms, your houses and fine places
But pity not the shanty boys while dashing on their sleigh
For around the good campfire at night we'll sing while wild
   winds blow
And we'll roam the wild woods over and once more
   a-lumbering go

[Repeat chorus]

Then when navigation opens and the water runs so free
We'll drive our logs to Saginaw once more our girls to see
They will all be there to welcome us and our hearts in
   rapture flow
We will stay with them through summer the once more
   a-lumbering go

[Repeat chorus]

When our youthful days are ended and our stories are
   growing old
We'll take to us each man a wife and settle on the farm
We'll have enough to eat and drink, contented we will go
We will tell our wives of our hard times and no more
   a-lumbering go

And no more a-lumbering go
We will tell our wives of our hard times
And no more a-lumbering go

THE LUMBERJACK'S ALPHABET

"The Lumberjack's Alphabet" was a favorite song in the camps, with each logger putting their own unique spin on the shanty. "P for Peerless" refers to the brand of chewing tobacco that was popular with the men.

A is for ax which we swing to and fro
B is for boys that handle them so
C is for cant hooks, the logs we make spin
D is for danger that we're always in

[Chorus]
And so merry, so merry, so merry are we
We are the boys when we're out on a spree
Sing "hi-derry col-derry, hi-derry-dum"
Give the lumberjacks whiskey and nothing goes wrong!

E is for echo which through the woods rang
F is for foreman that pushes our gang
G is for grinding stone, the axes we ground
H is for handle that turns them around

[Repeat chorus]

I is for ink which our letters we've wrote
J is for jacket we wore for a coat
K is for kindling, the fires we'd light
L is for lice that bothers by night

[Repeat chorus]

M is for money, which everyone owes
N is for needle that patches our clothes
O is for oxen the road we swung through
P is for Peerless, which everyone chews

[Repeat chorus]

Q is for quiet, when we are asleep
R is for rabbits which everyone eats
S is for sleigh, so stout and strong
T is for teams that tote them along

[Repeat chorus]

U is for use which we put ourselves to
V is for valley, we tramp it right through
W is the woods we leave in the spring
And now I have sung all I'm going to sing

BAND ON THE BALL

Formed in 1921, the Lumberjack Band was a marching band that played at the games of the Green Bay Packers, the NFL team from Wisconsin. They earned their name from rocking the lumberjack style in plaid mackinaw jackets, heavy boots, and hunting caps.

THE LUMBERJACK SONG

Perhaps the world's most famous wood-felling anthem, "The Lumberjack Song" first appeared in a 1969 episode of *Monty Python's Flying Circus*, featuring the iconic clip of cross-dressing logger Michael Palin, an increasingly concerned chorus of Canadian Mounties, and girlfriend Connie Booth, who bemoans: "Oh, Bevis! And I thought you were so butch!"

I'm a lumberjack and I'm OK
I sleep all night and I work all day
I cut down trees
I eat my lunch
I go to the lavatory
On Wednesdays I go shopping and have buttered scones for tea.

I'm a lumberjack and I'm OK
I sleep all night and I work all day
I cut down trees
I skip and jump
I like to press wild flowers
I put on women's clothing and hang around in bars

I'm a lumberjack and I'm OK
I sleep all night and I work all day
I cut down trees
I wear high heels, suspenders, and a bra
I wish I'd been a girlie just like my dear Papa!

OPPOSITE: A man wanders amidst the felled trees of the forests of Cowlitz County, Washington, 1941.

ABOVE: Members of Monty Python, and actor Tom Hanks, perform at The Concert For George at the Royal Albert Hall, London, 2002.

LUMBERJACK LINGO

If you want to live the life of a lumberjack, you'll need to know your pike pole from your peavey. Use these words and phrases to help you up your logging game. Yo-ho!

ALL HANDS AND THE COOK: Similar to the nautical "all hands on deck." Used to summon help for an emergency, such as a major log jam

AMEN CORNER: A place in the bunkhouse for storytelling

ANTIFREEZE: Any alcoholic drink

AXLE GREASE OR SKID GREASE: Butter

BAIT CAN OR BEAN CAN: A lunch bucket

BARKED: Someone who's lost their hair

BAR TOAD OR BAR FLY: Someone who spends lots of time in saloons

BEAN BURNER, BELLY-ROBBER, OR BOILER: A bad cook

BEAR STORY: A tall story

BEAR WALLOW: A dirty or untidy bunk

BEAVER: A clumsy axman, or a rough and uneven cut of wood

BETWEEN THE ROCK AND THE RIVER: Caught in a difficult situation with no chance of escape

BIRLING: Log rolling

BLACKJACK OR MUD: Coffee

BLANKET FEVER: An affliction suffered by lazy lumberjacks

BOILING-UP SHACK: A place to bathe or do laundry

BOOM: Logs chained or tied together end-to-end, used to catch and corral logs on the river

BOX UP THE DOUGH: To cook

BUCKER: Someone who saws trees into logs

BULL COOK: A boy who does chores around the camp, including feeding livestock and sweeping the bunkhouse

CALKS OR CORKS: Short, sharp spikes set in the soles and heels of shoes, used for better footing on logs during the river drive

CANT HOOK: A long pole with a thimble and a large, levered hook at the end, used to turn and roll logs

CHOKER SETTER: A logger who attaches cables to felled logs before they're hauled

COOKEE: A cook's helper

COUGAR DEN: A bunkhouse

DAYLIGHT IN THE SWAMP!: A saying used to wake up sleeping loggers

DEVIL'S CUP: A tin cup without a handle that becomes hot when filled with tea or coffee

OPPOSITE: These pikemen help logs navigate a sluiceway in Maine, 1943. Workers such as these helped prevent logs from getting stuck or creating any pileups. ABOVE: A logger attaches a choker loop to a log before a donkey engine winches it from the woods to the landing area in Cowlitz County, Washington, 1941.

DONKEY ENGINE OR STEAM DONKEY: A steam-powered winch used for hauling logs, operated by an engineer known as a "donkeyman" or "donkey puncher"

EPSOM SALTS OR IODINE: The logging camp doctor

FALLER: A lumberjack who cuts down trees

FLUNKEY: Someone who serves meals in the logging camp

FLY BREAD: Raisin bread

GABRIEL HORN: A tin horn used to announce meals were ready

GROUNDHOG: Someone who guides logs onto sleds

HASHHOUSE: The cookhouse

LOGGING BERRIES: Stewed prunes

LOG SCALER: The person who records the quantity and quality of felled logs before they're taken to the sawmill

MACARONI: Sawdust

MISERY WHIP: A crosscut saw, used by two lumberjacks for cutting trees

MONKEY BLANKETS, STOVE LIDS, OR SWEAT PADS: Pancakes

NOSE BAG: Cold lunch eaten in the woods

PASS THE 44S: Pass the beans

PEAVEY: A long wooden pole with a metal spike and pivoting hooked arm at the end, used to lift and turn logs on a river drive

PIKE POLE: A long wooden pole with a straight metal spike and hook at the end, used to control logs on the river and construct log rafts

ROAD MONKEYS: Crews that maintain logging routes and shovel the horse manure

SAWYERS: A pair of loggers who fell trees together

SHANTY BOY: A logger

SHANTY QUEEN: A logger's wife who lives in a rustic shack

ABOVE: During World War II, women worked at sawmills to help meet wartime demand for timber. This worker at a mill in New Hampshire rolls logs into a rack before they are run through a saw, 1943. **BELOW:** Buckers use a crosscut saw on a felled tree in Malheur National Forest, Oregon, 1942. **OPPOSITE:** Lumberjacks pose with a spruce log that they transported using a team of horses in the Cascade Mountains, Washington, 1905.

SHAPE UP OR SHIP OUT: What the boss says to lazy loggers

SHOEPACK PIE: A pie made from vinegar, cornstarch, sugar, and lemon or vanilla

SKIDDER: A heavy vehicle, used to transport felled trees from the logging site

SKOOKUM: A strong or brave man

SKUNK BIT: Stinking drunk

SNAKE ROOM: A room in a bar where drunken lumberjacks go to sleep off a hangover

SOUNDS LIKE A BUZZSAW IN A NUT: A heavy snorer

SWAMPWATER: Tea

SWEDISH FIDDLE: A crosscut saw

SWINGDINGLE: A sleigh for hauling food to loggers in the woods

TAR: Bad coffee

TEAMSTER: Someone who looks after and drives the oxen or horses used to pull logs

TIMBER: The warning cry of the faller, just before a tree goes down

TIMBER BEAST: Anyone who works in the woods

TIN PANTS: Heavy waterproof pants worn by loggers

TOP LOADERS: The highly paid and skilled men in charge of loading and hauling sleds

WHISTLE PUNK: The person who passes signals from the choker setter to the donkey engineer when logs are ready to be winched

WIDOW MAKER: A dead limb on a tree overhead

YO-HO!: Used to cheer on other lumberjacks at work or in competitions

WORD UP: American lumberjack, historian, and writer Stewart Holbrook wrote a handy Logger's Dictionary, published in his book *Holy Old Mackinaw: A Natural History of the American Lumberjack* in 1938.

BIBLIOGRAPHY

App, Jerry. *When the White Pine Was King: A History of Lumberjacks, Loggers, Log Drives, and Sawdust Cities in Wisconsin*. Madison, WI: Wisconsin Historical Society, 2020.

Atlantic Canada Tourism Partnership. Accessed March 30, 2021. atlanticcanadaholiday.co.uk.

Australian Axeman's Hall of Fame and Timberworks. Accessed March 30, 2021. thaiimperiallatrobe.com.au.

Beard, G. M. "Remarks Upon Jumpers or Jumping Frenchmen." *Journal of Nervous and Mental Disease* 5 (1878): 623–640.

——. "Experiments with the Jumpers of Maine." *Popular Science Monthly* 18 (1880): 170–178.

Beck, E. C., ed. *Songs of the Michigan Lumberjacks: From the Archive of Folk Song*. Recorded by Alan Lomax and Harry B. Welliver. Washington, DC: Library of Congress, 1960.

Burg, Rob. *A Taste of the North Country*. Last accessed March 30, 2021. atasteofthenorthcountry.wordpress.com.

"Canada Vignettes: Log Driver's Waltz." National Film Board of Canada. Accessed March 30, 2021. nfb.ca/film/log_drivers_waltz.

Center for Sustainable Economy. Accessed March 30, 2021. sustainable-economy.org.

Conlin, Joseph R. "A Social History of Food in Logging Camps." *Journal of Forest History* 23, no. 4 (October 1974): 164–185.

Cox, William T. Illustrated by Du Bois, Coert. *Fearsome Creatures of the Lumberwoods: With a Few Desert and Mountain Beasts*. Washington, DC: Press of Judd & Detweiler, Inc., 1910.

Curry, Kevin. Fit Men Cook. Accessed March 30, 2021. fitmencook.com.

Destination Canada. Accessed March 30, 2021. destinationcanada.com.

Discover New England. Accessed March 30, 2021. discovernewengland.org.

"Early Logging on the Menominee Indian Reservation: Life and Lore of the Menominee Lumberjacks." Menominee Indian Tribe of Wisconsin Historic Preservation Department, 2012.

Edmonds, Michael. *Out of the Northwoods: The Many Lives of Paul Bunyan*. Madison, WI: Historical Society Press, 2009.

Ellis, Charles. "Among the Michigan Pines." *The Chicago Current*, Vol. III, 1885.

Fitzmaurice, John W. *The Shanty Boy or Life in a Lumber Camp*. Cheboygan, MI: Steam Democrat Press, 1889.

Foat, Joanna. *Lumberjills: Britain's Forgotten Army*. Cheltenham, UK: The History Press, 2019.

Forest History Society. Accessed March 30, 2021. foresthistory.org.

Forest Stewardship Council (FSC). Accessed March 30, 2021. fsc.org/en.

Forestry and Land Scotland. Accessed March 30, 2021. forestryandland.gov.scot.

Fryeburg Fair. Accessed March 30, 2021. fryeburgfair.org.

Great Lakes USA. Accessed March 30, 2021. greatlakesusa.co.uk.

Hemsworth, Wade. "The Log Driver's Waltz." 1950.

Holbrook, Stewart H. *Holy Old Mackinaw: A Natural History of the American Lumberjack*. New York: Macmillian Company, 1938.

Johnny Appleseed Festival. Accessed March 30, 2021. johnnyappleseedfest.net.

Jones, Terry, Michael Palin, and Fred Tomlinson. "The Lumberjack Song." Charisma Records, 1975.

Kearney, Lakeshore. *The Hodag and Other Tales of the Logging Camps*. Madison, WI: Democrat Printing Company, 1928.

La French Sarah. Accessed March 30, 2021. lafrenchsarah.com.

La Drave. Directed by Raymond Garceau. Montreal: National Film Board of Canada, 1957. nfb.ca/film/log_drive.

A Famous Wisconsin Industry.

Laurel Fork Sapsuckers Sugar Camp. Accessed March 30, 2021. laurelforksapsuckers.com.

"Log Drive." National Film Board of Canada. Accessed March 30, 2021. nfb.ca/film/log_drive.

Lumberjack Beard Company. Accessed March 30, 2021. lumberjackbeardcompany.com

Lumberjack World Championships. Accessed March 30, 2021. lumberjackworldchampionships.com.

Maine Office of Tourism. Accessed March 30, 2021. visitmaine.com.

Melvin, J. I. "Foresters." *Meet the Members: A Record of the Timber Corps of the Women's Land Army.* Bristol, UK: Bennett Brothers, 1945.

Minnesota Tourism. Accessed March 30, 2021. exploreminnesota.com.

Muir, John. "God's First Temples: How Shall We Preserve Our Forests?" *Sacramento Record Union*, 1876.

"National Census of Fatal Occupational Injuries in 2019." US Bureau of Labor Statistics. Accessed March 30, 2021. https://www.bls.gov/news.release /pdf/cfoi.pdf.

New York State Woodsmen's Field Days. Accessed March 30, 2021. woodsmensfielddays.com.

Nova Scotia Tourism. Accessed March 30, 2021. novascotia.com

NYCitySlab. Accessed March 30, 2021. nycityslab.com

Pike, Robert E. *Tall Trees, Tough Men: A Vivid, Anecdotal History of Logging and Log-Driving in New England.* New York: W. W. Norton, 1967.

Simmons, Amelia. *American Cookery.* Hartford, Connecticut: Hudson & Goodwin, 1796.

Springer, John S. "Once More a-Lumbering Go / The Logger's Boast." *Forest Life and Forest Trees.* New York: Harper & Brothers, 1851.

Squamish Days Loggers Sports Festival. Accessed March 30, 2021. squamishdays.ca.

Stewart, K. Bernice, and Homer A. Watt. *Legends of Paul Bunyan, Lumberjack.* Vol. XVII of *Transactions of the Wisconsin Academy of Sciences.* Madison, WI: The Wisconsin Academy of Sciences, Arts, and Letters, 1916.

STIHL TIMBERSPORTS®. Accessed March 30, 2021. stihl-timbersports.com.

Sustainable Forestry Initiative (SFI). Accessed March 30, 2021. forests.org.

Sydney Royal Easter Show. Accessed March 30, 2021. eastershow.com.au.

Timber Lounge. Accessed March 30, 2021. timberlounge.ca.

Tourism New Brunswick. Accessed March 30, 2021. tourismnewbrunswick.ca.

Travel Yukon. Accessed March 30, 2021. travelyukon.com.

Tryon, Henry H. *Fearsome Critters.* Cornwall, NY: Idlewild Press, 1939.

Wild Axe Productions. Accessed March 30, 2021. wildaxe.com.

Wisconsin Tourism. Accessed March 30, 2021. travelwisconsin.com.

PICTURE CREDITS

ABOUT THE AUTHOR

Lauren Jarvis is an editor, writer, and photographer specializing in adventure, wildlife, and conservation. She has traveled extensively around North America and the world, enjoying such challenges as tracking grizzlies in British Columbia and trekking to Everest Base Camp. A regular contributor to National Geographic, Lauren is passionate about the planet's wild places and animals and loves spending time in the woods. Follow her on Instagram @laurenjarvistravels.

THE AUTHOR WOULD LIKE TO THANK

Darren Hudson at Wild Axe Productions, Nova Scotia; Stanley Scott, Nova Scotia; Hayward Meisner, Ironworks, Nova Scotia; Jethro Wood, Cloak & Dagger Tattoo Parlour, London; The Stihl Timbersports Press Team; Eben Lehmen, Director of Library & Archives; Finn Partners / The Brighter Group; Click Travel Marketing and PR; Travel and Tourism Marketing (TTM); US Forest Service; US National Park Service; Visit USA; Virginia Tourism; Travel Wisconsin; Walking Art Tattoos; Webster County; Woolrich. And her family . . . for helping her to see the forest for the trees.

"And into the forest I go, to lose my mind and find my soul"

JOHN MUIR

STERLING
New York

An Imprint of Sterling Publishing Co., Inc.

STERLING and the distinctive Sterling logo
are registered trademarks of Sterling Publishing Co., Inc.

"The Lumberjack Song" is written & composed by Michael Palin,
Terry Jones & Fred Tomlinson, issued under license from Universal
Music Publishing Ltd. on behalf of Python Monty Pictures Ltd."

ISBN 978-1-4549-4354-9

Distributed in Canada by Sterling Publishing Co., Inc.
c/o Canadian Manda Group, 664 Annette Street
Toronto, Ontario M6S 2C8, Canada

For information about custom editions, special sales,
and premium and corporate purchases, please contact
Sterling Special Sales at 800-805-5489 or
specialsales@sterlingpublishing.com.

Manufactured in Singapore

2 4 6 8 10 9 7 5 3 1

sterlingpublishing.com

Cover design by Melissa Farris
Interior design by Claire Stevens